Growing in Faith

Mission Possible

Ideas and resources for children's evangelism

compiled by

David Bell and **Rachel Heathfield**

Text copyright © 2000 CPAS
This edition copyright © 2000 CPAS
First edition 2000
Reprinted 2003

Published by
CPAS
Athena Drive
Tachbrook Park
WARWICK
CV34 6NG
ISBN: 1 902041 05 4

Printed in conjunction with
Scripture Union
207-209 Queensway
Bletchley
MILTON KEYNES
MK2 2EB
ISBN: 1 85999 411 3

British Library Cataloguing-in-Publication Data
A catalogue record for this book is available from the British Library

Scripture quotations taken from the HOLY BIBLE, NEW INTERNATIONAL VERSION. Copyright © 1973, 1978, 1984 by International Bible Society. Used by permission.

CPAS and Scripture Union are grateful to all the people who contributed so generously to this book. They include Karen and Steve Beale, Jackie Cray, Dave Gatward, John Hattam, Fliss Henderson, Steve Hutchinson, Ewan Jones, Simon Marshall, Sarah Mayers, Philip Mounstephen, Frank Nelsson, Ems Rookwood and Ruth Wills.

Compiled by David Bell and Rachel Heathfield
Edited by AD Publishing Services
Designed by ie Design
Illustrations by Mike Kazybrid
Printed by Unigraph Printing Services

Church Pastoral Aid Society
Registered Charity No 1007820
A company limited by guarantee

Contents

HOW TO USE MISSION POSSIBLE

'Mission?'

'Hmmm. Possibly.'

If that's how you feel about evangelism with children, then welcome to *Mission Possible*. This resource provides ideas for sharing the good news of Jesus with children and young people aged 0 to 14. If you are thinking about evangelism with children, it aims to get you started doing it. If you are already getting your hands dirty it provides creative ideas to help keep your work well thought out and fresh.

Mission Possible is meant to be used alongside the companion books in the 'Growing in Faith' series: *Children Finding Faith* by Francis Bridger and *Bringing Children to Faith* by Penny Frank. Together, they aim to give a thorough 'head, heart and hands' introduction to children's evangelism.

Note: The term 'children' is sometimes used in the text to refer to all those aged up to 14. This is for the sake of conciseness. In work with those aged 11–14 use a term such as 'young people' or 'younger teenagers'.

Finding your way round

In *Mission Possible* you will find two kinds of ideas page:

Using... (pages 10–21)
These cover six settings for children's evangelism with basic advice, points to consider and some starter ideas. Look through these to help you choose the best strategy to use in your situation and then get going with it.

Ideas for... (pages 22–60)
The main part of the resource is a miscellany of ideas for use in children's evangelism. Each idea has an age-group indicator and icons to show the settings where it might be most suitable. The ideas are divided into five sections based on the aims of the activities. They work through:

- getting ourselves ready for evangelism
- building relationships with children
- introducing them to what God is like
- telling them the good news of Jesus
- giving opportunities for appropriate responses.

Use ideas from all five sections to help you get a balanced strategy for evangelism. Beware of attempting shortcuts.

Getting the most out of Mission Possible

Where to use it
The six areas covered in the first part of this resource are not the only settings for children's evangelism. In particular you may want to consider using it for:

- **regular church groups.** The week-by-week work with children and young people can also be the main focus for evangelism. This has the advantage of putting evangelism at the heart of our children's work. It also recognizes the consistent, long-term nature of children's evangelism – building relationships, and gradually helping children to discover the good news of Jesus and to respond to it. However, it is important that we don't lose sight of the need to reach out to children outside the church. Find ideas for use in regular groups by looking for the 'children's home groups' icon.

- **residential activities.** Taking older children and young people away for a weekend, or going together to an organized residential activity (such as those run by Scripture Union or CYFA Pathfinder Ventures) is excellent for evangelism. There's so much more time to grow natural relationships and to explain the gospel. Many of the ideas in this resource can be adapted to a residential setting.

Make it work for you

The ideas in *Mission Possible* are meant to be a starting point. Work at adapting them to fit your situation, yourself, the team you have available and the children you are working with. Be creative.

Age-groups

Do not feel restricted by the age-group indicators next to the activities. They are meant only as a quick way of spotting ideas for your age-group. An activity shown as 0–4 may well be good for a 3-year-old but not a 1-year-old. You will know the young people you are working with best. The division of children and young people into four age-ranges for the resource is also arbitrary. You may well want to have events for 5–10-year-olds all together. Or you may run a 6–8s group or organize a party for the 11–14s and under-4s combined.

Children as evangelists

As part of getting children and young people involved in sharing their faith with their peers, get them to select the ideas in *Mission Possible* which they think would be good for their friends. Either pick some out and offer them as suggestions or give older children or young people the book to look at for themselves.

Follow-up

Where children are hearing and responding to the good news of Jesus, we have a huge responsibility laid on us – to nurture their faith. Often that will be through our regular church children's groups, or we may set up children's home groups specifically for the purpose. Usually in those groups we will have children at different points in their growth in faith all mixed together. We may, in effect, be running a 'just looking', 'Christian basics' and 'going deeper' group all rolled into one. In fact an individual child may well be in all three categories at once.

Whatever point the children are at, we need to be doing the same basic tasks: building good relationships with them, showing them Christian faith lived out, helping them learn from the

Bible and giving opportunities for them to respond to God in appropriate ways. Ideas from *Mission Possible* can be used as a basis for a follow-up programme – for example see the programme outlines in Chapter 4: Pass on the message (pages 45-52).

Key to icons

 church services

 family events

 children's home groups

 special events

 holiday clubs

 schools work

MEET THE CHILDREN AND YOUNG PEOPLE

Under–4s

Jackie Cray

Most of us are not used to associating the idea of evangelism with very young children. But if evangelism is to share the gospel of God, help people to learn about the ways of God and encourage them to be active followers of God, what could possibly exclude the under-4-year-old? They learn mainly through experience; through watching and copying who we are and what we do. They like to do things alongside us; to play and experiment. Sharing the gospel with young children is about discovering God through relationship and through their natural awe and wonder about creation and the world around them.

Under-4-year-olds are vulnerable and dependent on adults for nurture and care. The naturally appropriate way to share the good news of the gospel with young children is in an environment that includes their family members or carers, e.g. toddler groups, playgroups, toddler services, parenting support groups, thanksgiving or baptism services, all-age services.

Children are spiritual beings, created in God's image with a spiritual hunger to know him. In fact, when children are very young it is the most natural time to nurture their faith, to let them experience, alongside us, living in relationship with God, talking about him as part of our everyday lives, praying, loving, reading about him in the Bible, asking questions and being part of the church community.

Young children are experts in being dependent – in receiving all they need. That was the quality Jesus commended his adult followers to imitate (Luke 18:17).

4–6s

Ems Rookwood

'I am five. I can jump and run. I can hop and skip a little, but I'm not very good yet. I can throw a ball, but I cannot catch or kick it well. I have grown about 4cm this year. I can nearly always dress myself and tie my shoes. I can brush my teeth and hair and wash myself. I am learning how to read and write lots of short words. I can rhyme and can clap and sing a little.

'I am learning how to make friends. I like playing with other children, except when they pinch me or take my ruler. I miss my family when I am at school and sometimes I cry, especially when I feel poorly or hurt myself. Sometimes I want to go home before the end of school.

'I know that God is big and that he made the world, even elephants. We sing songs about him at school. Sometimes we sing to Jesus and sometimes to God. It depends. I got worried today when I went to the toilet because I remembered that God can see everything. I can pray to God. I don't like closing my eyes. That's stupid. I like to hear stories from the Bible, but some of the names are hard to remember. My favourite one is about the boy who took his lunchbox to Jesus. I've got a lunchbox. It's got an Action Man on it. Peter has got the same one.

'I asked my teacher where babies come from. She said that when a Mum and Dad love each other, they have a special sort of cuddle. Babies are like people but they have smaller ears.'

7–10s

Simon Marshall

Children seem to work in a mode of enthusiasm and wonder by default; they don't need much prompting to get excited about something which interests them. They are also seekers for truth: they want to find out about how things really work, why things happen and why people do the things that they do. The task of telling children about Jesus and what he has done for them may be made a little easier because they already have a desire to hear.

The child's world balloons out between the ages of 7 and 10. There are opportunities and pressures of school with tests, friendship groups and expectations from parents and other adults. Children of this age begin to look to other adults outside the family for support and affirmation; figures such as teachers, organizers of leisure pursuits and media personalities begin to influence the child's thinking and behaviour. Children also look more and more to each other to gain information and form ideas about life; peer groups become intensely important and strong ties will be formed between friends.

According to John Westerhoff a child aged between 7 and 10 will be in the 'affiliative' stage of faith. Here, stories, experiences of awe and mystery and feelings provide a sense of belonging for children. Activities which focus on creativity and sharing will help to deepen their faith. Much of the practice of their faith will be copied from other members of the faith community. They need to belong to it and participate in its life.

11–14s

Philip Mounstephen and Ewan Jones

Young people aged 11–14 are making important steps in developing a worldview; they are asking, and answering, some fundamental questions about why things are the way they are. This is why evangelism with them is both possible and essential.

This is an age at which the peer group is particularly important. Young people are struggling with all kinds of questions of identity. Increasingly they see themselves as individuals rather than as part of a family. But often the family is substituted by a peer group that provides a sense of belonging and of acceptance.

The unchanging gospel remains gloriously relevant to 11–14s. To those who are unsure about where they belong, Jesus says, 'You belong with me, you can be at home with me.' To those who have problems accepting themselves, Jesus says, 'I accept you, I love you, just as you are.'

Young people aged 11–14 are people of passion – of ambitions, dreams and goals. They are at an age when they are (or should be) discovering their talents and gifts. This is sometimes referred to as 'adolescent idealism'. Christian young people want to use what God has given them to make a difference in his world. If we recognize the gifts and goals that they have, and if we nurture their enthusiasm for the gospel and for Jesus, then they can be effectively encouraged and set free with confidence to share their faith.

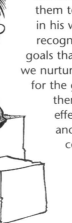

BEFORE YOU START...

'Children are people, too!' It's sometimes easy to find ourselves thinking about children's evangelism – the plans, the strategy, the aims – and to forget that 'children' are individual people. Though physically smaller than adults, children have hopes and fears, questions and needs which are just as important. Children are vulnerable and precious to God – and we have a responsibility to their parents and to God to be thoughtful and prayerful and to demonstrate respect for them in our approach to evangelism.

Practical points

The physical safety of children and young people is paramount. Make sure that the rooms you are using are safe, clean and secure. Make sure you have enough adult leaders and helpers for the number of children you have in your group (if in doubt, check with your local Social Services office for guidelines). Check the exits and entrances and any other potential dangers. Fit a gate if necessary to make sure small children and toddlers can't escape. Taking children out on a trip raises extra safety issues. Work through these carefully, and inform and train the team beforehand (see pages 16–17).

If you run a holiday club or a regular group, you must keep a register. You need to know which children are in your care, particularly in the case of fire. You also should have some sort of registration or 'consent' form with a record of the child's full name, address, phone number of adult carer or parent, and any relevant information concerning the child's health (e.g. asthma, a nut allergy). It is helpful for at least one of your team to have a first-aid qualification. Know where the first-aid box is kept. Know the procedure in case of fire. Find out your church's health and safety policy on issues such as these.

Your church must also have a child protection policy (see Guidelines on page 9). Team members should be given training in this. The policy should include team members signing a declaration form and providing a reference. Do not assume that everyone in contact with the church is automatically suitable and safe to work with children.

CHECK IT OUT!
- Check safety of premises
- Train team in safety issues
- Check adult/child ratio
- Keep a register
- Follow your child protection policy

Children's needs

Children are individuals with social, emotional, physical, spiritual and moral needs. Some of them may have bad experiences of broken relationships and poor role models. When they are in our care, we have a responsibility to look after them. We need to offer a safe environment where children are welcomed, valued, listened to and respected. And we ourselves need to develop safe, wise and good practice in our work with children.

Our relationships with individual children need to be genuine and appropriate. We need to listen carefully to children, and be sensitive to their needs. But we also need to make sure that our one-to-one contact is healthy, secure and unambiguous (see Guidelines on page 9).

Listening is an important skill, which sometimes needs to be learned. It helps to get down to the child's level and make eye contact, communicating face to face. Learning names quickly, remembering details of what the children tell us and referring to them again helps build relationships. And our use of language is important – talk in language children can understand, and use concrete examples. Above all, be yourself and be genuine. As appropriate, demonstrate your own faith, and pray for the children you meet.

We also need to be aware of how the children relate to one another. It might be that children who do not normally mix are together in a room. Be aware of issues of racism, bullying or teasing that might arise. Try to act to defuse problems before they happen.

LISTEN!
- Relax and be yourself
- Make eye contact, at child level
- Learn names, be interested in the child's interests
- Think about your language level
- Listen with your ears and your eyes
- Pray for the children you meet

Child protection

Your church should have a child protection policy – if not, get one! It is extremely important that you work from this document, or under guidelines from your diocese or supervisory body. This policy should set out good practice for working with children, based on the Children Act 1989, including how to minimize the risk of abuse or allegation of abuse occurring within the church and what to do if you should hear of abuse. Make sure the church arranges training in child protection issues for all paid staff and volunteer children's workers.

Useful addresses

If you do not have a child protection policy, contact your diocese or supervisory body for help. The following organizations also offer help:

The Churches' Child Protection Advisory Service, CCPAS, PO Box 133, Swanley, Kent, BR8 7UQ (Tel: 01332 667207/660011). The CCPAS advises and supports churches on issues of child abuse and child protection, providing workpacks and training materials.

NSPCC, 42 Curtain Road, London EC2 3NH (Helpline: 0800 800 500). NSPCC provides helpful leaflets on abuse and prevention.

Kidscape, 152 Buckingham Palace Road, London SW1W 9TR. This is a charity campaigning for children's safety.

Childline (Tel: 0800 1111) – a free 24-hour helpline for children. Consider advertising this in your church.

Your local Social Services department will also advise you on issues of child protection. Their number will be in your local phone book.

GUIDELINES FOR GOOD PRACTICE

Careful planning helps good practice. The following points will help you think through certain aspects of your children's work, but they are not a substitute for your own church's child protection policy. These guidelines are taken from and based on the Home Office report 'Safe from Harm', following the Children Act 1989, and are for the protection of both children and those adults who work with children and young people.

- When possible, try to have at least two adults with a group.
- An adult should not be alone with a child where there is little or no opportunity of the activity being observed by others.
- Where children are transported by car, try to have more than one passenger in the vehicle.
- Respect a child's right to personal privacy.
- In a counselling situation with a young person where privacy and confidentiality are important, make sure another adult knows the interview is taking place, and with whom.
- Make sure that the level of physical or verbal contact is appropriate.
- Remember that someone else may misinterpret your actions, however well-intentioned.
- If you see another adult acting in ways which might be misconstrued, be prepared to speak to them or to another leader.
- Make sure you know what to do in suspected or disclosed cases of child abuse.

USING CHURCH SERVICES

Possible shapes

Your church may provide for any or all of the following types of service:

- main services – time when all ages are together
- all-age services
- services focusing on a particular age-range (e.g. youth services, children's praise services, toddler services)
- services for non-churchgoers (e.g. seeker-friendly)
- services marking special events (e.g. Christmas: Christingle, crib and carol services; Easter, or church anniversary or dedication festival)
- services linked to another event (e.g. the climax of a holiday club, or the day after a special family event).

Things to consider

You need to look at what you are already doing and make it more effective for reaching children and their families:

- Is the whole congregation warm and welcoming to children?
- Is the crèche warm and friendly with a high level of care for children and parents?
- Does the service leader introduce and explain things clearly and in a non-patronizing way? Will newcomers, young and old, feel lost in the service pattern or will they be guided gently through?
- Are services shaped only by tradition and habit (ancient or more recent) or do you adapt to fit both the people you have and the people you are reaching out to? How do you help everyone own this process?
- How do you use activities, symbols and sacraments so that they help people of all ages?

Hospitality and welcome

- When will a new family be shown or told about what is where (toilets, crèche, children's groups, refreshments)?
- Who is responsible for welcoming? The whole church may be very good at this but

someone other than the minister needs to make sure it is happening consistently. Give welcomers training (see ideas in Chapter 1, Get set! on pages 22-28). Make sure there are enough welcomers so that this is done properly (or perhaps have extras on standby for busy times).

- What are your refreshments like? Are they as good and as well presented as you would give visitors to your home? How do people get them? Do you need to make them more easily accessible or even bring them out on trays at the end of the service? Are the refreshments good for children? How do you expect children to enjoy the refreshment time?
- Many newcomers will feel more confident if they know how long a church service will last. If you have stated an end time, build trust by trying to stick to it.

Invitations

- Do you introduce couples coming for marriage to other couples in the church aiming to build relationships? Are you letting them hear about your faith and see it in action as part of marriage preparation? When they have children do you invite them to your parent and toddler group? What do you do for children already around at the time of the marriage?
- If children have been brought for thanksgivings, dedications or baptism, but later stopped coming, do you keep inviting them and their parents to services and events from time to time? How can you help them to make relationships in the congregation?

First ideas

- Have a sheet of basic information about coping with the service. You could include: Why do we meet? What happens in a service? Who's at the front? What happens for children – when and where? Do we need to join in? Where and when do we get refreshments? Where are the toilets?
- Run an optional crèche facility for every church service. This should be a retreat for parents struggling with noisy babies and toddlers – not a way of showing they are excluded. Crèche helpers should see chatting to parents as part of their role.
- Use this pattern for an all-age service talk relevant to everyone:

    1. Retell the Bible passage even if it's just been read. (You could use pictures or a question-and-answer format.)

    2. Make the point of the passage simply. (Word it so a 7-year-old will understand. You could link in an activity or illustration.)

    3. Suggest applications relevant to different ages and situations ('So when we're at nursery…, or when the boss at work…, or if our next-door neighbour…').

    (Scripture Union's *SALT: All ages* contains plenty of resource material for all-age talks; see page 61 for more details.)

- Check that the people involved at the front of the service are representative of the congregation and area, e.g. all ages, male and female, different educational backgrounds, different races. Opportunities include: prayers and readings, interviews and testimony, teaching activities, drama. Also include leaders the children will recognize from their groups and activities.

For the whole church

This approach to children's evangelism is the most challenging in that it requires change from all members of the church. But without it, children who are taking their first steps of faith can find themselves feeling excluded instead of part of a new all-age family.

Try to think how to meet the needs of existing church members at the same time as being a place where new children and adults are comfortable and are introduced to the good news of Jesus in an accessible way. If that is done by having separate seeker-friendly services, the whole congregation needs to be helped to own them. If it is decided to make the main service more accessible, it will take a lot of honesty and love in talking and praying through any changes with the whole church. The whole church family can be involved in prayerfully expecting and welcoming newcomers.

Why not…?

Under 4

Plan a simple, 20-minute toddler service. If you already have a parent and toddler group, it could be a regular (e.g. monthly) add-on to the group time. Clear a space for parents to sit on the floor. Sing some lively songs with simple actions and words. Tell a Bible story using as much visual input as possible. Perhaps make something to remind them of the story. Say a simple prayer and then have some refreshments. This is a good opportunity for ministers to get involved and meet parents.

4–10

Some churches are finding the *Kidz Church* material very useful. It was designed by Bill Wilson who set up a children's church in the Bronx, New York, gathering unchurched children for a time of teaching and worship using video, music and games. The material provides everything you need for the presentation. It is currently distributed in the UK through Kingsway Publications, Eastbourne.

11–14

Enable young people to design and present their own service. Give them a theme and let them think about and rehearse a drama, some singing and some prayers. This service could happen in the normal church building or elsewhere and it could be just for them and other young people or for the whole congregation.

USING FAMILY EVENTS

Possible shapes

The basic strategy for any family event is for church members to bring non-church families along with them. Each event will need something interesting and engaging for each age-group – although don't expect every event to appeal to every taste. The main aim is to get families and the church family doing an activity together. (For further information on how to draw whole families into Christian faith, see *Families Finding Faith*, published by CPAS and Scripture Union.)

Indoor events

- **Café bar with family quiz or family challenge** – in big enough teams so families can stay together but work with others.
- **World food evening.** Have a cookery event where food representing different countries is ready to be cooked or prepared by a number of families. Make sure there is enough for all ages to get involved with: peeling, mixing, chopping and stirring. Then all sit down and share the different tastes together!
- **Church open day.** Provide activities to watch or try out in different corners showing what goes on in the life of the church.
- **Sales.** These could include: attic, bring and buy, car boot, sales of work, exhibitions, auctions. Or go for a traditional fayre with side stalls as well.

Out-and-about events

- **Walk.** You could organize something local led by an expert on the history of the area, or go to a beauty spot. Have an incentive to keep people going – such as a cream tea at the destination.
- **Sports or games activity.** Organize traditional races and team games but with a particular family feel. Make sure all shapes of family, and those who have come alone, are included. For example, have a 'Dads and Daughters' race – but the dad and daughter don't have to be related to each other. You could hire a sports hall or swimming pool.
- **Treasure or scavenger hunt.** Team up non-church families with their church friends and set them off to find the treasure from cryptic or photographic clues. Use as big an area as possible. Or get everyone scavenging for silly objects.
- **Photo hunt.** Give a list of things to find and photograph in their teams – maybe the whole team in a phone box or lying in a line, head to toe. Give the teams disposable cameras, and set a finishing deadline that gives you enough time to take them to a one-hour processor while the teams have tea together. Enjoy the pics.
- **A trip out to a local attraction.**

Things to consider

- Does the event you are planning appeal to the families you want to be there? Does it fit in with your neighbourhood? Is it the sort of event your church families would like to bring their friends to?
- If your hope is that church members will invite families they already know, how is the church enabling normal and natural relationships to grow and develop? How much time do people have for this, given their other commitments? Do you need to find a radical way to cut down on the meetings some church members have to come to?
- What will your publicity be like? How can you advertise it to children in a way that they will want their family to come? How can you do the same for adults?
- Think about the people on the fringes of church involvement. Will this event draw them closer into the church and into relationships with Christians?
- What message do you want these families to hear? Do you want them to hear that the church and Christian people are fun so that they might come again and then hear about Jesus? Do you want to tell them something about Jesus at their first event?
- What future events are you planning? How does this one fit into the programme? How will you use this event to invite people to other events and to your regular church activities?

First ideas

- **Make a skills list.** Ask around the church and find out what skills, hobbies and areas of knowledge there are. Also find out about any access people have to places of interest through their work or other activities. Include people on the fringe as well as those who are already seen as leaders. Use the list to brainstorm ideas for events using people's strengths. Their enthusiasm and skill will make all the difference to running a good event.
- **Have a play corner and play leaders available** for points where younger children want to do their own thing. Be realistic about their concentration spans and capacity for being organized. Make sure they can take part in the main activities, but also provide them with an extra place to let off steam.
- **Use a PA system unless the event is very small.** This will help those who hear less well not to miss anything. It also makes it possible for everyone to hear what young children say, e.g. you can do a TV-style interview of the winners of the 'Dads and Daughters' race. Bear in mind the older people who will be part of the event in every aspect of the planning.
- **Provide food at any event** – have a barbecue, pancake bar, doughnuts, cakes or biscuits. Food is a great way of showing welcome and hospitality.
- **Do a review of the event,** asking one or two people of different ages what they thought. Write down their answers – even if they don't agree with your own point of view – and relay them to the rest of the team when you are planning the next event.

For the whole church

- Church members must own the event. This will be easier if they have the date early and can make it a priority.
- Choose the planning team carefully, involving a cross section of ages and interests.
- Encourage people to come and support the event as much as you dare. It is vital this encouragement comes from the church leadership. The congregation must sense that evangelism is high on the church agenda.

USING CHILDREN'S HOME GROUPS

Possible shapes

Children's home groups can comprise a wide range of types:

- choice of content (Christian basics or 'Just looking', Bible-study based, or questions-based)
- timing (weekly, fortnightly, monthly, after school, Saturday lunch, Sunday tea, a continuing group or a short course, e.g. six weeks)
- occasion (preparation for baptism, membership, confirmation or communion, or a follow-up to a one-off event for those who want to dig deeper into faith)
- age-groups (mostly for those over seven years old, but also parent and toddler daytime groups)
- ideally less than ten members
- single-sex or mixed group.

Things to consider

- How are you going to get a group of children together? Do the children you already know want to bring friends? If you are starting from scratch, what is the first point of contact with the children?
- What will you do when the group gets above optimum size (say, over fifteen)? Have you got more leaders for another group? Are you praying about this yet? Plan for growth.
- Who will lead the group? How can you make sure they are able Bible teachers, not just those who are willing and have spare time? Do you need to plan the timing so the right leaders are available, rather than the other way round?
- How will you share the vision for the home group with the church?
- How will you support the leaders? Who are their 'line managers' and how will they carry out that task?

First ideas

- **Choose a good venue which is comfortable** – in the home of a leader or group member, or a room at church. A church member might be willing to host the group without actually leading it. Meet round a kitchen table or in a front room.
- **Put together a relaxed and informal programme** to include some or all of the following: food, some input and prayer, games and a simple response activity. Aim to be together for around an hour.
- **Be *very* careful about child protection issues.** These apply as much in a home as on church premises, and perhaps need even more care in an informal setting. Make sure that the ratio of adults to children is always appropriate.
- **Let the group decide their own name** – it might relate to who goes and when it happens, or where it meets.

For the whole church

- Plan who will support the group in prayer. You might be able to create a link between an adult group and the children or young people's home group. Or ask individual adults to take on a commitment to pray. Provide them with information and progress reports so that their prayers are informed.
- If your church runs adult home groups, your children's home group could sometimes follow the same programme – adapted in an appropriate way. This would help the group to feel part of the church, and help parents and children to talk about what they are doing in their groups.
- Work on how to link the home group members in with the life of the wider church. For example, agree to meet for breakfast one Sunday and go to the service together. Or give the group a task to do within the life of the church. Could the children be welcomers, do the prayers or reading, or even lead part of the service? Could they help make and serve the refreshments?

Why not...?

Under 4

Try a weekly group for parents and under-4s which meets once a week at lunchtime. Aim it at parents who are wanting to find out more about God and the Christian faith. Provide food or agree that you will each bring your own. Other church members who are available in the daytime but who do not have small children could help provide food.

Have a limited aim of what you will achieve – for the parents a Bible reading and a sheet with two or three interesting questions to chat about and take home; for the children an activity such as painting, craft, cooking, which leads into a retelling of a Bible story and brief prayer before they go home. Have good Christian children's CDs and books to play and look at each time. Don't see the children as a distraction from any adult chat – this is a drip-feed approach. Parents may later feel confident to go to another group where they can explore things in more depth, and children can move up into the regular church groups.

7–10

- Have a food activity – make pizzas, have a fondue, decorate biscuits, make cakes.
- Build relationships by having a home group sleepover. Make sure girls and boys are in separate rooms and that you have adults elsewhere in the house. Tell parents clearly about these arrangements from the start. Have plenty of food and some good videos to watch.
- Use *My Place in God's Story* by Rachel Heathfield and Simon Smith (CPAS) as teaching material.

11–14

- Use *Youth Alpha,* or *Sound Foundation* (published by Scripture Union, a youth-friendly introduction to Christianity in the form of a five-week course).
- Have a 'Simpsons' night. Choose an episode, watch ten-minute chunks, draw out the spiritual themes and discuss.
- For relationship building, have a fast-food crawl. Go round as many fast-food outlets as you can, buy one portion of chips at each, share and score out of ten.

USING SPECIAL EVENTS

Possible shapes

Parties

- bouncy castle or ball pool
- graffiti walls
- traditional party games and party food
- parachute games
- quality crafts
- have a theme and link a short gospel message to it

Sports events

- traditional sports day with physical and mental challenges to suit all children
- *It's a Knockout* event with silly challenges, wet and dry
- hire a small sports hall or swimming pool

Going out

- trips out: to the beach, the zoo, a theme park, a farm, skating, bowling or go-karting. These are especially good where parents don't take their children on such trips. The church may need to subsidize some trips to make them attractive.

Specials

- Set up a coffee bar or café in your church for the whole weekend. Encourage your church children and young people to get involved decorating and planning, and get them to invite their friends along. Put on a programme of live music, clowns, short talks, craft activities and games.
- Hold a nightclub event. Have a DJ, lights and plenty of dance space. Have a non-alcoholic bar with weird-sounding drinks and a tuck shop.
- Use festivals throughout the year as a reason for celebrating: Alternative Valentines, Pentecost Party, Good Friday workshop, All Saints Hallelujah Party or Christmas Ball.

Things to consider

How does this fit into your overall plan for evangelism with children? If one-off events suit you best, should you run a series through the year to grow and build relationships and trust? If so, how can you link those events together clearly with a logo or event name?

Where is the best venue? Can you use the church building as a way of introducing children to it, or will another venue be better? Are there any community buildings or spaces? Have any of your contacts got a suitable property – a farm, a pool, a field?

Who is it for? Do you aim to invite every child you have contact with, or just a particular group? Do you want to limit the size, e.g. for a smaller trip out? How will you publicize the event?

How can you get your children and young people involved in the planning of the event? How can you make it something they want to bring their friends to?

First ideas

- **Produce clear and attractive publicity.** Make sure that the church's name is on posters and invitations, and give a contact number for parents' questions about the event.
- **Produce a 'safety sheet' for team members highlighting any safety issues for the event.** This is especially good if you are going on a trip. Include safety in transport, road-crossing, staying in groups, first-aid procedure, what to do if a child gets lost, and places which are off-limits. There may be further safety factors specific to the place you are visiting – check these out on a planning visit. Also communicate this information verbally to the team at a planning meeting before the event, with time for them to ask questions.
- **On a trip, have a couple of team members on duty at an obvious point which you can show the children when they arrive.** This is the place to go to if they lose contact with their group leader.

For the whole church

- If you have a special event on a Saturday, you could invite the children to a special service the following day. Prepare the church family to welcome them. Refer in the service to the special event in as many ways as you can.
- Use the gifts and time of church members to help in preparation and planning, delivering invitations, making food, providing transport and prayer.

Why not...?

Under 4

- Have a teddy bears' picnic. Invite children to bring their teddies to a good picnic spot. Play some games (Musical Teddies – hide them when the music stops) and tell a story involving a teddy.

- Go on a train trip together. The destination could just be a nice place to eat a picnic and play outside for a while before returning home.

4–10

- Hold a circus skills workshop. You could include face-painting, clowning, juggling, plate-spinning, balloon-modelling and unicycles. There might be someone local to you who will come with all the equipment and give lessons. If not, you should be able to find people who can teach juggling, do face-painting and learn balloon-modelling. Add in any other interesting skills of any sort which your church members or contacts can share. This is good for involving parents who would not otherwise come to a church event.

- Have a drama or music workshop. Use the skills of the members of the congregation to put on a play or learn some new skills.

11–14

- Have a chocaholics event – play chocolate games, have a chocolate fondue, have chocolate cooking and chocolate prizes. If chocolate doesn't appeal, try a different food event: a barbecue, a pancake evening (with savoury and sweet fillings) or an ice-cream factory (provide ice cream and all the bits to make a variety of sundaes).

See *DIY Celebrations* by Nick Harding (CPAS) for ideas for events through the year.

USING HOLIDAY CLUBS

Possible shapes

Begin by thinking about the following key points:

- timing (e.g. summer, half-term, bank-holiday weekend, mornings, afternoons, all day)
- content (you could use published holiday club resource material such as Scripture Union's *Go for Gold* or *Megaquest*, see page 61). Alternatively, adapt regular group material, or produce your own home-grown material.
- offer a play scheme as an act of Christian service to the neighbourhood.

Things to consider

A holiday club takes quite a lot of organization. Start planning at least six months in advance.

- Who is it for – church children or non-church? Should you focus on reaching a particular area, school or estate (while not excluding others)? How will you do publicity? What is the best venue? How many can it hold? Will this affect who it is for?
- How will you keep in touch with the children you meet at the club? Is this the one evangelistic event you will have in the year? Or will you be inviting them to come on to other events, to your regular children's work or to a children's home group?
- If you want them to come to regular children's work, is that group or activity suitable? Will it need to change? Will an influx of non-church children compromise the aim of the regular group or strengthen it? Where will you find leaders for that?
- How can you use the best practice, skills and experience from the regular children's groups in the holiday club? How can you use the strengths of the holiday club in the regular children's groups? Will that take extra effort and resources?
- What is the budget for the event? What process does this have to go through so that the church will underwrite the project? How else will the church leadership support the event?
- How are you going to make contact with the parents of the children? Should you plan a special event or service at the end of the club?

First ideas

- **Think imaginatively about a venue.** Ideally, go for somewhere which will accommodate your preferred programme, but be realistic and, where necessary, adapt the programme to the building available. Think big and be flexible! Consider a marquee, a local school, or the church building with furniture cleared. Be willing to work hard to make the venue attractive, e.g. putting up posters.

- **Get as many children as possible to register beforehand.** This makes the arrival and welcome procedure easier on the first day. Set a limit on the numbers of children who can come. This will be in accordance with fire and safety regulations of your building as well as the number of leaders you have.
- **Always stay within the guidelines of your church's child protection policy** (see pages 8–9), including having a signed declaration form and reference for each team member. Arrange child protection training for the team. In the UK, the Children Act requires a holiday club to be registered with Social Services if it meets for more than four hours a day over more than six days in the year.
- **Some clubs have teaching-related activities in the morning and off-site activities on certain afternoons.** Is there somewhere you can visit that would echo the theme of the week – a fire-station, a farm or the zoo

perhaps? Otherwise, you might simply want to go to the park to play games and sports. Afternoon activities like this could be optional extras.

■ **Have funsheets, activities or craftwork to take home.** These can help children remember what they have learned, encourage continuing response and also communicate with home about what you are doing at the club. Make sure that what goes home is clear and concise, e.g. include a key verse or story summary on a fun sheet.

■ **Have an event or service for parents to come to at the end of the club.** Include drama, singing, displays of craft work and any other contributions the children have put together during the club. Give a flavour of what you have been doing. Provide refreshments or food. Have church people there with the specific job of welcoming and talking to new families.

For the whole church

■ Prayer is vital. Ask someone closely involved with the club to be prayer secretary, creating prayer letters and cards and distributing them to people who will pray. Each team member could be asked to find two people who will especially pray for them and the children they work with. Keep the whole church informed of prayer needs (while remaining sensitive to issues of confidentiality), and be creative in getting them to pray.

■ A holiday club provides many ways to get different people involved. Have a list of jobs to be done and try to recruit outside the realms of the people normally involved in youth and children's work. Use people's special skills for workshops or to give practical help. Include older teenagers in ways appropriate to them as individuals.

■ Get the whole church to come to the event or service at the end of the club.

Why not...?

Under 4

Think about having a shorter programme for this age-group each day. It could meet on fewer days, too.

Have at least a little time with all the age-groups together, e.g. for some singing or a brief activity. For the rest of the time, if possible, use a different area in your building for the younger children. Make this space very attractive for them.

4–10

For some of the time use age-related small groups with the same leaders each day. Encourage group identity, with a group name and a group den or corner. This will help you manage the children and encourage co-operation in activities. Leaders will also build better relationships more quickly.

Re-run popular activities throughout the club so that children don't miss out – and for the fun of it.

11–14

Have a separate programme for this group. This could be at a completely separate time and with a very different feel. Include one or two social activities.

Try doing some or all of each teaching session in a location appropriate to the day's Bible material, e.g. Palm Sunday – walking down a (traffic-free!) road; Gethsemane – in a garden; Jesus' death – on a hill; the resurrection – in an upstairs room or on the beach, if appropriate.

USING SCHOOLS WORK

2+2=4

Possible shapes

Building a good relationship with your local school is a very important part of a whole-church strategy for evangelism among children and young people – after all, it is where they spend most of their time. However, it is not simply a case of strolling into a school and saying 'We're from the church...' The relationship between the church and teachers (particularly the head) needs to be a trusting and honest one. They need to be sure of your motives and sure that what you want to do is in the best interests of the children and in keeping with the school ethos. Make sure that you build this relationship carefully and over time, so that the church is associated with good relationships and quality activities rather than difficult and weak ones. Consider the following:

- Start up a lunchtime club or help a Christian teacher with an existing one. A club like this will serve to support church children and to reach out to others. Clubs need to be lively and fun to compete with break time.
- Start a Christian Union or prayer group. This would primarily support Christian children and young people but would also provide an excellent base to do outreach and evangelism with the group members.
- Put on an event over a number of days with a number of different events, groups, talks and discussions that children could come to and hear about Jesus.
- Set up a gig with a Christian band or theatre group.
- Lead assemblies. If you can, do this regularly to become a familiar figure to the children and young people. Be careful about how much you say with an overtly Christian content. You must be sure that the headteacher agrees with what you are going to include. Say 'Christians believe...' rather than stating things as fact.
- Help with Religious Education. All schools have to include RE on the curriculum. Some put all their RE input in a concentrated block of one week. If you have already established a good relationship with the school this is an ideal opportunity to serve the school and help children hear what Christians believe.

Things to consider

Where do you already have contact with schools? The key to working in schools is a good relationship. Work on any existing contact and treat the relationship with care. Be careful that everyone involved is sensitive to the issues. One mistake can spoil the relationship and lose a lot of carefully won good will.

Which school(s) do you want to start building relationships with? Begin by writing to or visiting the head. Be clear about what you are willing to offer and for what purpose. You might begin by suggesting input into assemblies or offer help with RE. If you offer something, be sure that you can deliver it in a competent way.

Which church members are concerned about schools and will pray with commitment? If you are going in to a school 'cold', make sure you have people praying for you and for the early relationship with the teachers you meet. The potential for working in schools is vast; you need God's strength and wisdom as well as protection from spiritual attack.

In some places, there is a link between church attendance and securing a place at a church school. This can help with the relationships at school and can also bring more children to regular church groups. How can you make the most of this link? How can you build relationships with these children so that they stay after they get in to the school? Would a group at the school or an after-school club be a better way to keep contact?

Generation to Generation (published by Scripture Union) contains further helpful information on building up schools work (see page 61).

20

First ideas

- **Make a club or group as regular as possible.** It will only run in school term time so make the most of the time available.
- **Support and pray for any Christian teachers at the school.** They might have been waiting for some outside help before starting something, and so might want to work with you. But do not be offended if they are too busy to help practically.
- **Find out about lunch arrangements before you set up a club.** Be flexible and understanding, and use the time you have to the full – perhaps 30-40 minutes.
- **For an after-school club, provide a drink and biscuit** and an opportunity for children to sit down for a quiet few minutes, should they want to.
- **Set up a regular consultation with any church children who are at the school.** Use their knowledge and experience, involve them if they want, and make sure you do not embarrass them in anything you do at school.
- **Make sure the group programme is lively and attractive;** have lots of high-energy games and fun.
- **Leave any room you use exactly as you found it.** Get the children to help.
- **Think of a name for the group.** It can be clear that it is a Christian group without having the word 'Christian' in the title. (One school has a club called 'Splat!')

For the whole church

- Make sure you have prayer support. There might be a group of parents willing to pray regularly for the school as a whole.
- Encourage and enable the children and young people in your church groups to be evangelists, bringing their friends along. However, be very aware of how costly it is for some children in some schools to declare their faith publicly. Do as much as possible to help them in this. Pray for them.
- Think about the possibility of the school group members joining a church group if they want to find out more. However, do not think of schools work as simply a recruiting campaign for church groups. It is a ministry in its own right.

1 GET SET!

IDEAS FOR CHANGING OURSELVES TO BE READY FOR EVANGELISM

The ideas in this section will help prepare you and your church for evangelism with children. They help people to grow in understanding of children and their faith, to reflect on attitudes to children within the church and to make any practical changes needed so the church will welcome and nurture children growing in their faith. For a fuller treatment of this whole area, *Bringing Children to Faith* (published CPAS) is an essential tool.

• •

Sermon set

Aim: To help the adult congregation explore a biblical view of faith in children and adults

Ask the minister/church leaders to include in the teaching programme a short series of sermons looking at a biblical view of the faith of children and adults:

- 'Pass it on' (Deuteronomy 6:4-9)
- 'Fit to serve' (1 Samuel 3:1-21)
- 'First and last' (Mark 10:13-31)
- 'Relate. Right?' (Ephesians 5:21; 6:1-4)

These could also be a series of studies for a Bible study or home group.

• •

Testimonial twins

Aim: To help the church discover how children respond to God

Introduce a regular instant interview feature at all-age worship. Ask one child or young person and one adult the same two questions: firstly 'What would you like to thank God for at the moment?' and a second question determined by the theme of the service. Allow the two people to prepare their answers beforehand, offering help to think through their answers.

Pray briefly for these two individuals.

• •

Hospitality check

Aim: To make any church group or situation more welcoming

Ask a group of leaders to brainstorm together answers to the question: 'If someone visits your house, how do you make them feel welcome?' Get all the suggestions you can, relating to guests of any age. After writing up the ideas, work through them thinking creatively about how you could apply each one in your church or group situation. Some may not fit – that doesn't matter. The point is to see what practical measures make children and/or adults feel welcome, and to put some into practice. So you might decide to have some toys out ready for small children or offer adults good tea or real coffee when they arrive or... Be willing to be radical to put the needs of visitors first.

You could go on to turn the ideas into a Welcome Charter – a set of points saying how each person visiting the group or church will be welcomed. You might produce one for each age-group.

Children's representative

Aim: To ensure church leadership structures take children into account

Have someone on the main church leadership body with a specific brief to represent children and to bring up issues relating to them. That group itself – church council, elders, leadership team or whatever – will need to agree the best way to do this, for example co-opting someone who will do the task well, or delegating a present member of the group to take on the role. The person chosen should:

- make sure the leadership body has agreed its aims for children's work in the church and considered the practical implications, e.g. if we want more children, how will we free up (and train) good leaders and provide space for activities, and do we need to change our services?
- raise any topics of particular concern or relevance to children
- point out where any other topic under discussion has an impact on children as part of the church body.

(There is also a need to make sure older teenagers' views are represented. This will often be best done by directly including one of that group in the leadership structure.)

Blast from the past

Aim: To help church leaders or team members think about the nature of children's faith

Ask each person to bring along an item which is a reminder of something or someone which influenced their growth in Christian faith as a child. Alternatively they could simply bring a photograph of themselves as a child.

Take it in turns to explain the objects you have brought and say something about where you were in relation to Christian faith as a child and what events or people influenced that faith. Some may tell the story of how their faith developed. Others may say they had no faith as a child but will be able to talk about influences then which have an impact on their faith today.

Discuss: Is there a danger that we expect most children's experience of faith to be like our own (e.g. a gradual response, a moment of conversion or no response until adulthood)? What can we do to understand children's faith experiences which are different from ours?

Pray for each other, thanking God for bringing you all to faith in Jesus.

THINK!

'If anyone causes one of these little ones who believe in me to sin, it would be better for him to have a large millstone hung around his neck and to be drowned in the depths of the sea.' Matthew 18:6

Actually, the 'little ones' in Jesus' warning covers his followers of all sizes and ages. We are all vulnerable to things which could trip us up in our faith. As we get going on evangelism with children we need to shift any chunks of rock lying round for them in our churches. Things like...

- not recognizing that children can have real faith
- sidelining children's needs in services or other events
- being passive rather than active in our encouragement (hoping they soak it all up without too much effort on our part)
- avoiding getting to know them because they are too demanding
- not encouraging their gifts.

The bigger the block, the more effort and pain there will be to move it.

I am, therefore I need

Aim: To help a leadership group plan for children's needs

Produce a flipchart or overhead projector sheet divided into three columns with the following headings:

- I am like this... ■ Therefore I need... ■ Why not...?

Define the age-group of child you are considering for this exercise. Ask group members to suggest characteristics of children of that age-group and write these in the first column. Then, for each characteristic, ask what implications this has for the church's provision for that age-group. Write these in the second column. Finally, ask for practical suggestions of how you could meet these needs more effectively. Write these in the third column.

Part of one church's chart for a 4-year-old might look like this:

I am like this...	Therefore I need...	Why not...?
Have a short/variable attention span...	*Short activities – freedom to spend short or long time on activity*	*Make things more flexible – free movement between activities for some of the time*
Think in terms of immediate world	*Talk in terms of things in their world*	*Have an event where they bring things along from home? Jim to think about what, how, etc. Sharing news time – link to prayers?*
Feel safer among familiar things	*Not too much change*	*Change back from rota system for this age-group to having a more regular team? Ask Edna.*
		Structure each group session in the same way?

With people who have a fair knowledge of an age-group this exercise can be done in pairs with the same chart produced on handouts.

● ●

Love out

Aim: To reflect on God's love and be motivated to share that love with children

This reflection can be used by an individual or a group. Read Psalm 103. Pause and think over the words, remembering how God has shown his love to you personally.

Think of a child you know well, e.g. in your family, friends or church. Pick out words and phrases from the psalm which speak to you particularly powerfully of God's love for that child. If you are in a group, invite anyone who wishes to say these words and phrases aloud and write them up.

Think of a child who is outside your church family at the moment – one whom you do not know well or that you find difficult. Read John 3:14-17 as a reminder that God's love is for all people. Reflect on the phrases, and remember that God's love is just the same for that child as the one you know well.

In a group discuss your responses to these questions:

- How can we show God's love to the children who are already inside our own circle of love and friendship?
- How can we show God's love to those who are outside that circle or on its fringes at the moment?

● ●

First impressions

Aim: To improve the church's welcome to new families

Ask a family who have never been to the church before to come along specifically so they can give you feedback on how welcoming you are. Ideally ask a family you know with at least two children of different ages. Choose the right people and they will enjoy being asked for help.

Afterwards visit the family to get their views on what made them feel welcomed and what did not. Make sure you get the children's feedback too. Bring what they say to a meeting of the appropriate church leaders to discuss how you could make the church more welcoming. Use the following checklist and the ideas in Chapter 2, Make the connection (pages 29-36):

- arriving and coming through the door
- the start of the service
- through the service
- refreshment time
- the welcomers (is more training needed?)

You could test the welcome at a pram service, toddler group or 11-14's group in a similar way.

The question game

Aim: To get the team to think about the good news of Jesus and how to tell it to children

To prepare, write the following questions on cards:

- *(3-year-old)* If Jesus is here, how can he be with Grandpa too?
- *(4-year-old)* Is Jesus a swear word?
- *(5-year-old)* Is heaven scary?
- *(6-year-old)* What's a Christian?
- *(7-year-old)* Did Jesus want to die?
- *(8-year-old)* Does God love bullies?
- *(9-year-old)* How can I say 'yes' to Jesus?
- *(11-year-old)* How can I be good enough to be a Christian?
- *(12-year-old)* Have you got the Holy Spirit?
- *(13-year-old)* How can I believe Jesus came alive again?

Place the shuffled cards face down. Ask team members to take turns at picking a card and asking the question of another group member of their choice. The person asked must suggest how they might answer it to someone of the age given. They then have the next turn at picking a card and choosing who will answer it. Encourage the whole group to chip in with suggestions – make sure it does not feel competitive. Alternatively people could work in pairs.

At the end, look through the questions again and ask if anyone wants to comment on the answers given – whether to clarify the content of the gospel or to discuss how best to explain it to children of different ages. You could agree to do further research on some areas using books or asking other leaders in the church.

You could adapt the questions to focus on one age-group.

Culture vulture night

Aim: To find out about children's cultures

Have a team session devoted to experiencing the cultures of the age-group of children you are working with. Do some research beforehand to find out what TV programmes, videos, food, music, games, websites and so on they enjoy. Don't assume you know without asking them. There may be several different cultures represented amongst your children – reflect all if possible. Put together a fun evening's programme of trying out as many of these things as possible. Have plenty of things set out to look at and try out – CDs, computer games, magazines, their top website. Have a break for food and drink and to watch one or two of their top TV programmes.

If you work with 11-14s, be sensitive. They may not like the feeling of being investigated so involve one or two in planning the evening and 'educating' the team.

Finish with a time praying for the children now you've absorbed something of their cultures.

Church check-up!

Aim: To help a leadership group think through current provision for children

Ask a leadership group to consider the following statements, and for each person privately to rate them on a scale of 0 to 5 (where 0 means 'I totally disagree' and 5 means 'I totally agree'). Define what age-range you are considering.

My church is a place where children see good relationships being modelled.	0 1 2 3 4 5
The people in my church are aware of the stages through which children pass.	0 1 2 3 4 5
My church welcomes children well.	0 1 2 3 4 5
The language used in my church is accessible for children.	0 1 2 3 4 5
My church is a place where children feel that they belong.	0 1 2 3 4 5
A child who had never been to church would feel at home if they came to my church.	0 1 2 3 4 5
There are plenty of things happening at my church now which would help a child's faith to grow.	0 1 2 3 4 5

Share scores and work out a total for each statement. For the three lowest-scoring statements, agree specific action to take. You could try out the questions on some church children, too, to get their views.

Thessalonica holiday club

Aim: To give team members a biblical view of evangelistic ministry

Read the following letter or give out copies:

> *Dear Nan and Grandpa,*
>
> *I'm having a great time on holiday. I've been to the 'Jumping for Jesus' Club at the church here every day. There's a leader in our group called Paulette and she's top. Whoever does the biggest smile gets to sit next to her. She makes us laugh. We think she fancies the leader in the next group.*
>
> *We've been learning all about how much Jesus loves us. Today we had a story about a man who was horrible but Jesus forgave him. I had to climb up a tree. Paulette had been up half the night making it. I think she's perfect.*
>
> *Two more days to go. Paulette won't be there on Friday cos she's going away with some friends for the weekend. She's taken my address so she can write to me when I get home.*
>
> *Love and kisses,*
>
> *Josie*

Ask the team members to rate Paulette (out of 10) on the following aspects of children's evangelism:

- relationship with children
- communicating the good news
- hard work
- right motivation

Swap scores, explaining your reasons.

Read 1 Thessalonians 2:1-13 for Paul's example of ministry. Discuss:

- What things from these verses is Paulette getting right?
- What areas might she need to work on?
- What encouragements are there for her? (Notice God's part in verses 2, 4, 12, 13.)

Individually choose a verse or phrase from this passage to remember. Suggest that people write these out and put them up somewhere at home.

Said and done

Aim: To encourage the church or team to pass on the good news

Give each person a piece of paper and a pen. If possible, sit in a circle. Read Psalm 78:1-8, which speaks of passing on to the next generation all the great things God has done and said. Ask each person to write on the top quarter of their paper something great which God has done from the Bible. Fold the top over to cover the writing and ask them all to pass the papers round to the right until you say 'stop'. (If this is being done with a sizeable congregation the passing will be more chaotic – just make sure that everyone ends up with a different piece of paper.) Now ask everyone to write down on the next section of paper something God has said from the Bible. Repeat the folding and passing on. Next, all write down something which God has done for you personally – which you don't mind others knowing. After folding and passing them on again, ask each person to write out Psalm 78:4 on the last section. They may then open them. Finish by thanking God for the things he has done and said. Get people to take away the papers they ended with for their own encouragement.

● ●

The full story

Aim: To help the team grasp the Gospel accounts of Jesus and respond to them afresh

Together watch a video version of the life of Jesus: *Jesus of Nazareth*, *The Jesus Video* (available from Agapé) or *The Miracle Maker*. Afterwards pray for the children you will work with – to grasp who Jesus is and what he has done for them. Pray for each other as you seek to follow Jesus.

For a low-tech version, read right through Mark's Gospel in an evening. Ask three or four people to work together to prepare and practise it.

Family connections

Aim: To help church leaders assess children's experiences of being part of the church

Ask a few children of different ages to answer the question: What do you most like about being part of (*name of church*)? Record their answers on a camcorder. Avoid them hearing each other's answers by using a quiet corner for your mini-studio – a chair and a camcorder on a tripod. Repeat this with the question: 'What do you least like about being part of (*name of church*)? (If you will be able to edit the video you could ask each child both questions and separate out the answers afterwards.)

Play the video to the church leadership group. Ask them to discuss what things currently happen in the church which help children to know they are part of the faith community. What more could be done? Think radically about: the structure of services, all-age events, children's participation in services, music, prayer, before and after services, involvement in home groups, informal social mixing within the church.

You might want to give some brief explanation on the importance to children's faith of being part of a faith community using the ideas in one of the other two books in this series (e.g. on the 'experienced' and 'affiliative' stages of faith development).

Burger consultation

Age: 11-14

Aim: To find out about young people's worldviews

In evangelism we need to help young people to ask the big questions about life – and to find answers in the Bible. But first we need to know how they are answering those questions at the moment.

Take four young people out for a burger or pizza (or whatever they would prefer). If possible, include an 11-year-old who doesn't profess to be a Christian, another who does and a similar pair aged 14. Sit them down and ask them the four basic questions – the answers to which make up our worldview:

- Who are we?
- Where are we?
- What is wrong?
- What is the solution?

Afterwards write down as much as you can remember of what they said. Use it as you shape your evangelism. As we help young people to ask the big questions about life and to find answers in the Bible, we need to know how they are answering those questions to start with.

THINK!

'Be imitators of God, therefore, as dearly loved children and live a life of love, just as Christ loved us and gave himself up for us as a fragrant offering and sacrifice to God.' **Ephesians 5:1-2**

The most significant way we 'share' who God is with our younger brothers and sisters is to be the sort of people who actively pursue bearing the family likeness. This means we need to develop a hunger for God's word, learn more of the Bible stories and work on our prayer lives and our whole-life worship of God. We must want to tell our stories about how God has worked in our lives. If we are apologetic, or unconvincing about our faith, we will produce a generation that is hardly interested in Christian things, lacking in conviction. We reproduce who we are as much, if not more, than what we say, particularly with the very young.

Fact-finding

Aim: To see that children's evangelism is possible, and to explore strategies for it

Ask two people to visit another church to see what they are doing in children's evangelism – this could be to a specific group e.g. a 7–11's group or holiday club, or it could be to talk to leaders there about their whole strategy for children's evangelism and to see it in action. If possible, get them to take a camera and tape recorder along to gather material to help report back to others in the church.

Alternatively send out several pairs to see evangelism in different settings – schools work, holiday club, all-age seeker service, and so on. If you do not have appropriate contacts in other churches, ask around other church leaders or get in touch with an organization such as Scripture Union or CPAS.

Discuss what was seen as a starting-point for planning your own strategy.

● ●

Prayer with hindsight

Aim: To pray for children realistically

Ask people to suggest what, with hindsight, they would like someone to have been praying for them when they were a child. Write up the suggestions and pray for the children in your locality and church using the suggestions to spark off ideas for prayer.

THINK!

Of course, good evangelism is done as part of the whole work of a church. It is part of its mission into the community it serves: one of the results of good evangelism is that new members will be brought into the body of the church family. To help this to happen, we need to ask ourselves if our church is a place which will help children to grow as Christians. There is little point in preparing a programme of outreach, organizing and advertising events, recruiting leaders and helpers, and then going through the hard work of running events if there is nowhere for the children to belong to and to grow at the end of it! We may sow some seeds, but we want to be able to nurture them too. We need our churches to be places where children are welcome and will be understood. This will involve not only those who are doing the evangelism being aware of these issues, but also those who are part of the church into which children will come.

2 MAKE THE CONNECTION

IDEAS FOR BUILDING RELATIONSHIPS

Good relationships are essential in children's evangelism – as the context of sharing the good news of Jesus and as the only way of effectively communicating what it means to live for him. Some of the ideas in this section will help you to get to know new children for the first time. Others will strengthen existing relationships with children and their families.

In print Age: 0-10

Aim: To get to know children's names

To prepare, make printing blocks of all the letters of the alphabet (upper and lower case letters). You could use cheap potatoes – cut them in half and with a small sharp knife carve the letters in mirror image on the flat white part. Alternatively cut letters out of thick card, or a couple of cheap mouse mats and stick them on yoghurt pot bottoms or blocks of wood so that the mirror image side shows. Identify each stamp by writing the letter the right way round on the top.

Give the children posters to print their names on and decorate. To get a good paint coverage put paint on sponges in saucers and press the stamps on to them. Don't start the children all doing their names at once as there will be heavy demand for some letters.

Graffiti names Age: 0-14

Aim: To get to know children's names and build group identity

Cover a large area with paper, e.g. strips of plain wallpaper or lining paper. Provide pens, paint and large brushes. Ask each child to write their name as a big design and then colour it in. If a leader or child is good at graffiti-style writing, they could do the outline of all the names and then each child can design the pattern to go inside. With young children a leader should write the names clearly.

Dial P for pizza Age: 0-14

Aim: To get to know children's names

Give each child a small piece of pizza dough – ready-made pizza and scone mixtures are available if you don't want to make your own. Provide a good array of the usual pizza toppings (e.g. cheese, tomato, mushroom, ham, pineapple, baked beans, pepperoni). For an older age-group have a few weirder toppings or colour some with dye. Ask everyone to make a pizza in the shape of the first letter of their name with whatever toppings they like.

Top tracks Age: 0-14

Aim: To get to know more about each other and give a feeling of group ownership

In a group that meets regularly (from toddler group to youth group), let the people who come take it in turns to provide the tape or CD which plays while they have refreshments. Give them a chance to say what it is and why they like it. This works especially well if the music chosen sometimes has specifically Christian content – with an opportunity for the person who chose it to explain why it's important to them.

Badge revelations

Age: 0-14

Aim: To chat while being creative and discover more about each other

Make badges using modelling material such as salt dough (see recipe on page 37), DAS, clay or papier mâché. Set a theme such as 'Not a lot of people know this' (facts about themselves) for older young people or 'Favourite things' for younger children. Allow the material to dry-harden, and paint in bright colours. Use proper badge pins available from art shops. For safety, a leader should attach these to the badges with superglue.

You can also hire or borrow badge-making machines which produce professional-looking badges from the children's own designs. Simple card badges with safety pins on the back or even designs on self-adhesive labels can also be good as can designs done on a computer. If a leader is especially good at drawing or cartoons they could produce fun name badges for all the children beforehand.

. . . .

Picnic in the park...

Age: 0-14

Aim: To build friendships with children and their families

(… or indeed in a field, on a beach, in a barn or up a hill.) Invite children and their parents to a picnic. Choose a location and programme which will provide:

- a non-threatening location
- a chance for adults to talk to each other
- something for children to do
- something for adults and children to do together
- a way of showing hospitality.

For example, you might go to a park with a good playground and have some well-organized team games too. Encourage people to bring their own food, but provide one or two extra treats for everyone, e.g. a selection of cakes and fruit.

The same ingredients are good to include in any type of family relationship-building event. Other favourites to consider are:

- barbecue with bouncy castle or ball pool
- family quiz night
- treasure hunt
- barn dance
- walk – with different distance options.

Welcome team Age: 0-14

Aim: To welcome new people at church services

Set up a team of people with the task of welcoming anyone new at church services. Organize some training to agree the best way to do this so that visitors – children and adults – feel welcome but not overwhelmed. The team could include one or two children who would be good at welcoming other children. Members of this team could:

- greet people as they arrive
- make sure new children know about any groups for them, with information about what happens and an introduction to someone of their age
- chat to new people before and after the service
- have a welcome leaflet giving basic information about the church
- pray for people they have met and welcomed.

. . . .

A refreshing change

Age: 0-14

Aim: To use the refreshment time at services for relationship-building

Many churches serve refreshments after services. This can be a good time for children to grow friendships but for many, especially new children, it can be awkward or boring. Make the most of the opportunity by having something informal going on for the children to get involved with each week. You will need to plan what will work in your space. For example:

- a small but active game – *Twister*, skittles
- a video
- a puzzle sheet or wall quiz
- someone teaching juggling or another skill
- a building challenge (the tallest tower of bricks or longest bridge)
- table tennis or table football
- toddler play equipment
- child-friendly food.

Consider other changes to your refreshment time to help relationship-building too, such as carrying drinks round to people on trays so they don't have to queue, or breaking for refreshments in the middle of the service.

By special invitation

Age: 0-14

Aim: To invite children to an event

Produce invitations with a difference. The quality and effort put into the invitation will raise children's expectations of the event. Get a few adults and children together for a fun evening producing them. Here are a few suggestions to get your own ideas flowing:

- Cut shapes out of card or make a concertina of paper linked to the theme of the event, e.g. a foot, fish or frying pan. The basic design and information can be photocopied on to the cards first.
- Write the name of the event and a design on balloons using permanent OHP pens and add a tie-on label with the information about the event. Those invited can blow it up (you'll need to partly blow it up before writing to get the design dark enough – use a pump for hygiene reasons).
- Write a few words on biscuits or small cakes with writing icing – put the rest of the information on a paper wrapper.

Make sure invitations (or other publicity) include all the practical details with a contact name and number and a brief description of what will happen. Make clear that the event is organized by your church. If at all possible, personally name and hand-deliver invitations to all children with past or present church contacts.

Trad games Age: 0-14

Aim: To have fun, build relationships and get parents involved

The well-known, traditional games can still be very effective. For example:

- musical statues, bumps or chairs
- rats and rabbits
- stuck in the mud
- pass the parcel
- identify the baby photo
- balloon tennis
- scavenger hunt/Chinese laundry
- unihoc/shinty.

If you don't know them, ask around or get a book such as *Over 300 Games for All Occasions* by Patrick Goodland (Scripture Union). At a family event, parents can help run games such as these which are familiar to them, or older children can run them for younger children. Or try your own twists to the rules – unmusical statues (stop moving when the music starts); wrap the parcel (the prize starts wrapped in one layer of paper; when the music stops the person adds a layer of wrapping or a bag – the last one takes them all off again); identify the hair (photos of children and leaders when younger with only the forehead and hair showing).

Do you come here often?

Age: 0-14

Aim: To help the team get to know children

Some team members may be experienced at chatting to children, but others will find it does not come naturally and needs practice. At the informal times ideal for starting conversations it's all too easy to be diverted into other tasks and miss good opportunities for relationship-building. Come up with a list of conversation starters to use (get the team to brainstorm more) and practise them on each other. Make sure they lead to real conversations where you share information about yourself, too. For example:

- What have you enjoyed most today/yesterday?
- Have you ever been to … before?
- What is your favourite game to play?
- What things do you enjoy doing?
- Do you watch TV much? What do you like?
- Who lives with you in your house?
- Do you know the names of the others in the group?

Table time Age: 0-14

Aim: To build relationships and celebrate a festival

Invite the children to a special meal at Christmas, Easter or another festival. Prepare interesting looking food, e.g. sandwiches as mangers (cut off the crusts to act as legs) or pizzas spelling out 'JESUS'. Eat it as a sit-down meal together. With younger children plan some games and songs to use at the table. With older young people, have some good background music and plan one or two topics of conversation that will involve everyone. At the end have a reading of the Bible passage appropriate to the festival with only candles for light. (Take care!) With younger children, if possible, tell the story from memory or use a story Bible.

• •

Building site Age: 0-14

Aim: To chat while being creative and discover the impact of your church building

Alongside other activities on an occasion when a good mix of ages are present, work together to make a model of your church building using boxes, paper and paint. The bigger the better. Allow people to join in for as much or as little of the time as they want. As you do it, use the opportunity to chat about what people think of the building: How welcoming is it? How does it make you feel when you first come in? Does it reveal anything about the people who meet there – and why they meet?

Parenting group Age: 0-14

Aim: To support parents within the church and the community, and to build relationships

Set up a monthly parenting support group – invite parents of all the children you are in contact with. Produce a programme showing the venue (a home will be more relaxed), dates, topics and guest speakers. Being organized and having specific issues to tackle will encourage parents to feel it is worth coming. Topics could include: learning through play, making time for children, behaviour (good and bad), making the most of school, books and storytelling, introducing children to prayer, grandparenting. As guest speakers you could ask: a teacher, a nursery nurse, an experienced grandparent, a church children's leader, a child psychologist, a children's writer…

Have plenty of time for discussion and swapping ideas. Agree ground rules on issues such as confidentiality of what is said.

• •

Ransom notes Age: 4-10

Aim: To get to know children's names

Have a big pile of newspapers and magazines. Give everyone a blank sheet of paper, and provide scissors and glue. Ask the children to find the letters that make up their names and stick them on the sheet. They should then add any pictures or words they can find to say something about themselves and what they like.

THINK!

In the Old Testament, everyday family life was to be the main setting for passing on the faith to children.

'Impress [these commands] on your children. Talk about them when you sit at home and when you walk along the road, when you lie down and when you get up. Tie them as symbols on your hands and bind them on your foreheads. Write them on the door-frames of your houses and on your gates.'
Deuteronomy 6:4-9

How can we use the ordinary activities of life as the natural setting for sharing God with children today? It might be in a small group meeting in a leader's home, or children and leaders going away on a residential activity, or the growing friendship between a Christian and a non-Christian family. Helping parents nurture their own children's faith must be a priority.

Alphabetti-spaghetti

Age: 4-10

Aim: To get to know children's names and build group identity

Get into small groups. Give each group a plate and a tin of alphabet spaghetti tipped out into a bowl. Ask the children to spell out the names of everyone in their group on the plate. Have a time limit, say two minutes. Provide damp cloths for sticky hands. For a quick activity just use first names.

THINK!

If we plan to use special events such as family days or holiday clubs as a major part of our evangelism, we need to think carefully how to build up relationships with children who come…

- Special events need to be regular enough and attractive enough to get children coming back again and again.
- As children arrive, there should be something happening for them to get involved with alongside leaders who will chat to them.
- It helps to use small groups as much as possible, keeping the same leaders with each group.
- Alongside the special events there needs to be a regular group to nurture children who are ready for that step – a specially set up children's home group or the weekly church group.

Baked beans Age: 4-14

Aim: To have fun together

For this game, you'll need a bit of space and more than one leader. The children spread out at one side of the room. Call out different types of bean. For each one the children have to do a different action.

- runner beans (run on the spot)   *french beans   o la la*
- broad beans (stretch arms as wide as possible and puff out cheeks)
- dwarf beans (crouch down as small as possible)
- string beans (move arms in and out of one another as if tying knots)
- jumping beans (jump up and down on the spot)
- jelly beans (do an impression of a jelly using the whole body with sound effects)
- baked beans (run to the opposite side of the room. If they are tagged by the leaders before they get there, they are put in 'the tin', an area set aside for this purpose.)

Leave any children in 'the tin' until the next call of 'baked beans'. Alternatively, play until there is only one survivor. Develop the game by mixing the beans, e.g. broad jumping dwarf beans, and inventing your own.

River/Road Age: 4-14

Aim: To have fun together

Get the children into a single-file column along a line marked on the floor, e.g. a rope or line on a carpet pattern. One side of the line is the 'river' and the other is the 'road'. Ask all the children to jump on to the road side with both feet together. From now on, every time you call 'road' or 'river' the children must jump to the appropriate side without touching the line. Catch them out by repeating a call or yourself jumping the wrong way.

For a competitive game with older children, anyone who jumps at the wrong time, hesitates, touches the line or jumps too soon, goes to the back of the line. Set an alarm clock for the time limit. The one at the front when the alarm goes is the winner. To make it harder, when you call 'turn' everyone turns round so the person who was at the back is now in pole position.

• •

Fruit bowl Age: 4-14

Aim: To have fun together

Sit in a circle, with one person standing in the centre. Go round giving each child in the circle the name of one of four fruits: 'orange', 'lemon', 'apple', 'banana'. When you call out a fruit, children with that name must move to another seat. The one in the middle must try to get to a seat too, so that someone different is left in the middle. Shout 'fruit bowl' to get everyone running at once. With older children use stranger fruit names which are different each time you play, e.g. kumquat, cranberry, clementine, coconut.

Name bingo Age: 7-14

Aim: To get to know children's names

As the children arrive, write their names on slips of paper. Include leaders' names too. Screw up the slips and put them in a bag. Give everyone a sheet of paper with a blank grid on it. (Use a 4x4 grid for a group of sixteen or more, or 3x3 for a group of nine to fifteen.)

Ask everyone to go round and find out the names of others in the group, getting them to write their names in the boxes on their grids. When everyone has a complete grid, sit down and play bingo. Pull names from the bag one at a time and read them out. Each person should tick off the names as they hear them. The first to get a complete row across or down should shout 'bingo' and claim a prize. You could go on to see who is first to tick all their boxes.

• •

Spotty map Age: 7-14

Aim: To get to know more about each other

Have an enlarged street map of your area – the bigger the better. Help each child to find their house on the map and to put a sticker on it with their name on. Look at the map together and use further stickers to mark places which are significant for the group members, e.g. the park where they play, schools, favourite shops. Don't forget to mark on it where the event is happening and where the church is. In a school club setting, you could use a plan of the school site and immediate area. Again, mark the places which are significant to them as a way to talk about school life. To get started ask for their favourite and least favourite places in the school or area.

Can you guess? Age: 7-14

Aim: To get to know more about each other

Get each child and leader to think of a fact about themselves that most of the others do not know, e.g. 'My mum plays volleyball', 'I went to Alton Towers yesterday', 'I hate cheese'… Encourage them to be as creative as they can. They should write these down on slips of paper – leaders can help with this. Ask each person in turn to draw out one of the facts and guess who it is about.

• •

Fondue questions Age: 7-14

Aim: To get to know more about each other

Write out simple questions on slips of paper, e.g. 'How many people live in your house?' 'What's the best thing about school?' 'What's your favourite TV programme?' 'What's your favourite place?' Put the slips of paper in a bag. Have a chocolate fondue. If anyone drops something in the chocolate they must draw out a question from the bag and answer it. Use the questions and answers to spark off further conversation: 'Does anyone else watch "Home and Away"?' At the end take turns in drawing out the remaining questions and answering them.

Wide water hunt Age: 7-14

Aim: To build relationships by cooperating in a game and having fun together

Choose a location such as a country park with open spaces and woods or undergrowth. You will need to define the area you are using with no one to go beyond that. Play in any number of teams each with five to eight members and an adult leader to help. Each team needs a base marked by a large empty bucket stabilized by a brick in the bottom and paper cups. These bases should be out of sight of each other. Beforehand, hide around the area containers with about 5 litres of dyed water in each – at least as many containers as the number of teams. Make sure they are well spread so they are not closer to any one team's base.

Give the teams a set time (e.g. thirty minutes) to find the containers of water and then carry water back to their base buckets using only the plastic cups. Once water is found by another team they will have to choose their strategy – to run and use that supply of water and/or to look for further supplies nearer their base. Moving buckets and taking water from other team's bases are not allowed. Have at least one leader circulating to check buckets are not interfered with. The team finishing with the most water (measured with a jug) wins.

Afterwards have a picnic together or go back to a leader's house to relax and eat. This will be excellent relationship-building time.

THINK!

Evangelism with children is an attitude. As Christians, we are continually reaching out to people with the good news of Jesus simply by being who we are. Our very lives are vehicles for the gospel. Of course we will fail and need forgiveness but, by being us, we will show Christ to the children we meet.

There is a myth that hangs around in children's and youth work that we have to be 'trendy', young and totally in touch with the world of children's culture. This is not the case. Not at all. True enough, it can help to know about the things that children are watching and reading, the things they spend their money on. However, what children most want and need is real relationships with people who are interested in them and want to get to know them. Those people are you and me. We communicate the amazing news about the God who runs out to meet us on the dusty road – like the father in Jesus' parable – by being the people God made us to be.

Fire and water Age: 7-14

Aim: To relax together and to meet parents

Have a barbecue with lots of water games. Invite parents along for a glass of wine or fruit juice for the last half-hour.

● ●

Nameball Age: 4-14

Aim: To get to know children's names and build group identity

Stand in a circle. Throw a ball from person to person at random. Each person should say their own name as they throw. After a while, change the rules so you each say the name of the person you are throwing to. With older young people introduce weirder rules such as 'say the name of the person two to the left of the one you're throwing to' or 'say the name of the person you're throwing to backwards'. Get them to suggest further variations. With more space use a frisbee, inflatable banana or whatever. With young children use a large ball and roll it across the floor.

THINK!

'Belonging before believing' has become a buzz phrase in evangelism. Today, many adults come first to be part of a church or a smaller group (like an Alpha or Emmaus group) and then come to faith. It may sound woolly to some, but it isn't really: it's about reflecting the fact that God makes the first move to welcome us, and he accepts us without condition. We simply need to do the same towards others. It's also about recognizing the fact that today people are coming from a long way away: there's a lot to learn, a lot to cope with, so we need to give them space and time without pressure.

That means our regular children's and young people's groups need to have fuzzy edges. We need to treat people as if they belong even if they only come once. By getting to know and remember their names and keeping a record of their addresses we can invite them to things in the future. Treat people as if they belong and they'll feel they belong. And, in time, they will come (we hope and pray) to belong for all the right reasons.

3 LET IN THE LIGHT

IDEAS FOR INTRODUCING WHO GOD IS AND WHAT HE IS LIKE

The ideas in this section will help children to make their first discoveries about God. Exploring something of God's character is a good place to start with children who have no knowledge of him.

GOD IS THE CREATOR

Balloon baboon Age: 0-4

Aim: To introduce that God is the Creator of everything

Use modelling balloons to make a baboon or another animal. Deliberately make it go a bit wrong. Explain that making it is very difficult: 'Isn't it amazing that when God made the world, he did it right! He made everything out of nothing but he made it all to work really well and to have the right number of legs.' Look at pictures of God's creation – including baboons – in books. If possible, go outside and point out some of the amazing things God has made.

Cats, trees, you and me

Age: 0–10

Aim: To introduce that God is the amazing Creator

Give each child some modelling dough. To make your own, mix 1 cup of flour, 1/2 cup of salt, 1 cup of water, 1 tablespoon of cooking oil and 2 teaspoons of cream of tartar, plus a few drops of food colouring. When it's a smooth paste, put it in a saucepan and cook slowly over a gentle heat. When it comes away from the sides of the pan, take it off the heat, turn it out and cool. Then knead it. Make several colours. Keep the dough in airtight containers.

Ask everyone to make a cat, a tree, and then a person. Compare the results each time. With younger children allow them to make whatever they want. Comment that everyone's models were different. 'God created everything around us. Isn't it great that he made cats as they are and made trees like trees. Isn't it amazing that they are all individual – like our models. And isn't it great that he made people to be as we are – aren't we amazing?'

With the youngest children, you could do finger painting instead. Add a little PVA glue to ready-mixed paints for better results.

And it was dough Age: 4–10

Aim: To introduce God as the Creator who was pleased with his creation

Sit at a low table with an anglepoise lamp on it, and gather the children round. Put a sizeable lump of modelling dough in a shapeless lump on the table. (See the previous activity for a recipe.) Tell the story of the days of creation (Genesis 1:1 – 2:3), ideally from memory. Or another leader could read it from a clear translation or story Bible. At the same time, do the following:

Day 1 – switch on the light

Day 2 – put up a very big umbrella over the table

Day 3 – squash dough flat (sea) and make a flower

Day 4 – reshape dough into a big ball (sun) and little ball (moon) held up in the air

Day 5 – reshape into an octopus and a bird

Day 6 – reshape into a four-legged animal, worm and human

Day 7 – reshape into a big smile with two dots for eyes.

THINK!

In planning our evangelism it is important to think what aspects of God's character it is appropriate to emphasize. No, this isn't an argument for holding back on aspects of the character of God in our teaching. It is an argument for bearing in mind the issues children and young people are facing.

So to children who feel that no one is ready or willing to listen to them we need to tell them about the God who is always more ready to listen than we are to speak. And to young people feeling the pain of being on the edge of things – children no longer, but not proper teenagers either – we need to tell them that God has a heart for the marginalized, for those who find themselves on the edge (e.g. see Deuteronomy 10:18-19).

And so we could go on. If our evangelism is to be effective, we need to ensure that we give children a vision of God which is faithful to who he is, and appropriate to their situation.

· ·

The sound of creation

Age: 7-14

Aim: To explore the greatness of God the Creator

Read the story of creation from Genesis 1:1 – 2:3. Provide hand-held percussion instruments, and any other noise-making equipment you can find (e.g. household objects). Together work through the days of creation exploring different sounds and combinations of sounds to represent each one. Use voices and bodies too. If possible work on it, then try recording it and finally perform it to others with or without narration.

Foil face Age: 11-14

Aim: To understand what it means to be created by God

Give each person a piece of aluminium foil. Ask them to press it carefully over their whole face – making an impression of all their features from chin to forehead. If possible, spray the foil faces in a light paint colour. Later put them up and get everyone to guess whose face is which. Strong-angled light helps.

In an all-age setting, have a few prepared and leave them up as a quiz throughout the event. Every person will need a number or name badge to help with identification. For a more up-front presentation, get three people to make the foil faces beforehand and invite others out to guess whose they are.

Read Psalm 139:1-6 while you look at the masks. God made us all different, and knows us completely. There may be things we love about ourselves and things we wish were different, but God knows and loves us as we are because he made us.

GOD IS WONDERFUL AND HOLY

· ·

Flawless Age: 11-14

Aim: To introduce that God is holy and that his creation is spoilt

Collect items which look fine but are actually flawed. Through the first part of your event get the young people to try them out, e.g. ask one to put on a CD which doesn't work, another to pass you a cup where the handle comes off. Make the faults and problems bigger as the session goes on.

Point out that some things in life seem all right at first but later you find there is some fault or flaw. It's the same with people – even our greatest heroes are not perfect. Explain that you are going to read something written thousands of years ago – Psalm 145:1-5. The person who wrote it had found someone who was perfect. Then read the first line of verse 17 – 'The Lord is righteous in all his ways'. Explain that people today have discovered the same truth about God.

The Wow! factory Age: 0–6

Aim: To introduce that God is wonderful (based on Psalm 8:1-2)

Think of places where the children like to play. Turn different parts of your space into mini-versions, for example:

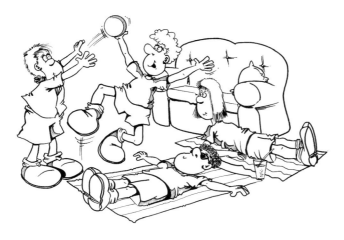

- nursery/playgroup/school – paper and paints, storybooks
- beach – sandpit with equipment
- park – indoor slide, seesaw
- garden – ball game, e.g. skittles
- home – play tent or house set up as home or with construction toys.

If space is limited, just go for two or three. Show the children these areas and let them play. Encourage them to move round.

Gather together and ask the children where they most like playing. Point out that you set out the room as a good place to play in. Then say: 'But do you know who made the whole world with such wonderful places for us to enjoy? It was God. We can't see God, but we can talk to him. We can tell him

how wonderful we think his world is.' Go round the different areas saying (perhaps together): 'Thank you God for … to play in. You are wonderful.'

Prince of Egypt Age: 7-14

Aim: To introduce that God is holy

Show *Prince of Egypt*, the feature-length animated version of the story of Moses (available at high-street video shops). Afterwards ask the children what they thought of it. Particularly get them to say how the film portrayed God. What did Moses discover about God when he saw the burning bush? Let them put the ideas in their own words. It might be appropriate for a Christian adult or young person to say something about their understanding and experience of God's awesome holiness.

GOD IS KING

Special places Age: 0-4

Aim: To introduce that God is King of everywhere

Provide a large selection of cushions, sleeping bags, pictures, toys, books and so on, and ask the children to choose items to make one part of the room into their special place. They could build walls out of boxes and furniture. If possible, put up photographs of the children.

Sit in the space. Explain that it belongs to you as a group: it is specially yours because you have made it how you want. Ask about other places special to the children (a room or corner at home) and to their family (the whole home, a holiday place). Explain that the whole world belongs to God. It's his place and he decided what and who would be in it. That's what we mean when we say God is King. Because he is a special King we sing songs that tell him how amazing he is. We tell and listen to stories about some of the amazing and special things he has done.

Kings and lions Age: 4-10

Aim: To introduce that God is the greatest King

Provide lots of equipment for making puppets, e.g. yoghurt cartons, paper plates, roll-on deodorant tops and ping-pong balls (both great for eyes), masking tape (you can paint over it), cardboard, paint, material scraps (especially canvas as it glues easily), string, wool, dowelling, garden sticks (beware of splinters), socks (old ones or buy cheap sports socks).

Ask the children to make a puppet each. You will need a king, several lions and several other people for a story you will tell (Daniel 6). Show them basic puppet structures such as the following but encourage them to try their own ideas:

- rod puppet – a piece of dowelling with a circle of card for a head
- finger puppet – a paper cylinder small enough to fit the child's finger
- sock or glove puppet.

Discuss what the king puppet should be like. What would he wear?

When the puppets are made, retell the story using a simple Bible version as narration. Act it out with the puppets as you go along. Then try it through again more slickly.

Explain that though King Darius was enormously powerful, Daniel knew that there was someone even more important. King Darius discovered that too. Like Daniel, Christians today have God as their King – and doing what he wants is the most important thing in their lives.

THINK!

Young children learn by copying and doing. We need to show them what God is like through our own lifestyle, prayer and worship. And that is also the way that older children and young people will see the reality of what we say about God. We need to ask ourselves: Where do they see us praying in a way which can be a model to them? Where do they see Christian love for those who are poor and weak? Where do they see lives which are lived for God – acknowledging that he is Lord and King?

Power to choose Age: 11-14

Aim: To explore God's kingship of all things

Beforehand, ask one (or more) young person in the group to make a quick video of their room at home – with a commentary about what's there. They could get a friend to help.

Show the video. Discuss what space the group members have where they can choose how things are. How would they change those rooms/spaces to make them exactly as they want?

Set up a chair as a throne. Explain that whoever sits in it rules the universe. Get them to take turns at sitting in the seat and saying how they would change things in the world. At the end place some candles round the throne and read Psalm 93.

If this activity raises any big questions (e.g. Why does God allow suffering? How do we know God exists?) write them up somewhere and agree to work on them on future occasions.

● ●

Megamemory Age: 4-14

Aim: To introduce that we belong to God and he will not forget us

Ask some children to bring along an item they've owned for a long time. Place these all in the middle of the group. Add further objects of your own (the more bizarre the better). With an older age-group have at least twenty-five objects. Encourage the children to look closely at them.

Take the items away and divide into pairs or small groups (with a leader if needed) to list as many of the objects as they can. Check the answers. Ask if anyone forgot to list an object which belongs to them. It's unlikely. Read Psalm 24:1. God is King of the world – that means everything belongs to him. And because we all belong to him – and always have – he will never forget us (Luke 12:6).

GOD IS THE PERFECT JUDGE

A matter of right and wrong Age: 11-14

Aim: To show that only God can judge completely fairly

Give the following scenario:

'Rhys's mum has a serious allergy to wasp stings – she has to take pills straightaway after one or she might die. One day Rhys's mum phones him from a friend's house, twenty minutes' walk away. She's been stung and needs the pills fast. As Rhys sets off to run there with the pills, he sees a bike outside a house. He borrows it. Later, Rhys finds out the bike belongs to Annette at his school. She has a foul temper. He's scared to return the bike, so he takes it to the tip. He tells his mum a friend lent him the bike.'

'Annette's dad promises her a new bike which is bigger with more gears. He can't really afford it, but she's so upset. The day before they go to the bike shop, Annette hears about Rhys saving his mum. She guesses what happened to her bike. She sets off furiously for Rhys's house, but then stops. She wants the new bike. She decides to keep quiet and hope the old bike doesn't turn up later.'

Ask each group member to rate out of ten Rhys and Annette on how well they behaved. Discuss reasons for those scores. Go on to discuss what makes an action really good or bad. Point out that it's impossible for us to judge completely fairly but God is the true judge of the world – he has set the rules of what is right or wrong and knows everything we do. One day he will judge the actions of everyone who has ever lived. Read Psalm 96:13. God has said he will punish people for what they have done wrong. But he still loves people in spite of the bad things they do. So he has done something to deal with the problem.

Who says? Age: 0-10

Aim: To show that God is in charge

Show a clip from a video appropriate to the age-group where someone is shown getting into trouble with a parent or teacher, e.g. 'Pingu' or 'Neighbours'. Ask the children 'Who says what Pingu (or …) is allowed to do?' 'Who says what you should do and what you can't do – at home, at nursery/school, in this group?'

Read the account of Adam and Eve and the snake from a story Bible (check it out with the original in Genesis 3), or tell it yourself, e.g. using simple spoon and sock puppets. Explain that because God made everything and everyone, he is in charge of saying what everyone is allowed to do. But a lot of people choose to ignore him. Read Deuteronomy 6:5 and explain that God most wants us to know and love him.

THINK!

Our children may have a lot of questions about God. We may provide the only place where they can begin to discover the answers about him and about themselves and the relationship which God longs to have with them. It is vital that we encourage children to ask questions and are not afraid to answer them, or at least to try, admitting when we just don't know. When we listen, we show that we value a child. A child's questions can also help us to gauge where they are in relation to God; they are a sort of spiritual 'thermometer'. It is worth spending time thinking through the issues that children ask questions about – perhaps make a list – and keeping some possible answers buzzing in your head.

You're the boss Age: 4-10

Aim: To show that God is fair and just

Play a simple game like River/Road (page 34). Ask a child to be the referee in charge of enforcing the rules – judging who has hesitated or moved wrongly and sending them to the back. Allow others to have turns at refereeing too.

Afterwards ask how easy it was to be the referee. Were all the decisions fair? If not, why not? Ask if anyone has ever made up a game of their own for other people to play. How easy is that to do?

Explain that God is the judge of the whole world. He is in charge of making up the rules and deciding who has broken them. When people do things which are wrong – like hurting others – it makes God sad. That's not what he wants and it stops people being close to him. When God judges people he is always fair and right.

GOD'S CONSTANT LOVE

• •

Love from God Age: 0-4

Aim: To see that God loves us

Talk together about how you can show you love someone. Talk about things you might say or do. Swap real examples.

If it is warm, have a paddling pool set up outside. You could make sure the children come with swimming costumes prepared to play in it. Alternatively, just kneel round the edge. Provide plenty of objects and explore whether they float or sink. What makes a good boat?

Tell the children about Moses' birth (Exodus 2) using a baby doll, a bowl covered with a towel as the basket and a shower curtain draped over one side as reeds. Make the point that God showed his love for Moses and his family by protecting him. Moses would grow up to show God's love to other people. And God loves us too – more than anyone else ever could.

• •

Living up to the label

Age: 4-10

Aim: To show that God lives up to his promises

Show a selection of items that describe what they do on the packet, e.g. toothpaste, paint, food, something electrical. Ask: Should we believe that what they claim is true? Read out what each one claims and then test whether or not it does what it says, inviting the children to help you out. You could finish with a huge box with extravagant claims on the outside containing a team member.

Show the children a box with the following labels: 'Will never run out.' 'Guaranteed never, ever to break down.' 'Works all day and all night.' 'Goes with you everywhere.' 'Bigger than you can possibly imagine.' After some build-up, open it to reveal a heart-shaped cushion (or similar object) with a label reading 'God's love' on one side and with Psalm 117 written out on the other. Explain that God doesn't come in a packet but he does live up to his promises – the Bible tells us all about them. Many people have discovered his love for themselves and tried it out.

Love lyrics Age: 11-14

Aim: To introduce what God's love is like

Compile a pop music quiz using recorded snippets of songs with the word 'love' in the title. Ask the young people in teams of three to write down the title and artist and spot the connection. If you need help choosing current music, you could ask a slightly older teenager.

Discuss what sort of love these songs are talking about. Is it always 100 per cent good? Do any of the songs talk about broken or spoilt love? Write down a few of the lyrics from the songs beforehand to refer to and read out.

Explain that God's love is always perfect. It is unspoilt and totally generous. It is never motivated from selfish desire and never gives up. Read some of the lyrics of Psalm 63 (e.g. verses 1, 3, 6-8) with background music, introducing it as a different kind of love song. Explain that you will leave the music playing at the end as time for thinking and prayer.

THINK!

Experience – how things feel – is very important to young people in our culture. Our evangelism needs to take experience, emotion and imagination seriously, as well as the mind. Effective, well-planned worship and prayer with children and young people can touch the heart as well as the mind, and may well be a very effective tool for evangelism. Use them well, and – along with an effective teaching programme – you'll be engaging the whole person. As Blaise Pascal, French theologian and mathematician, once said: 'The heart has its reasons which reason knows nothing of.'

• •

Theme parties Age: 4-10

You can adapt this party plan to different themes to teach about God. Ideas are given for two themes: creation and space.

1.00 p.m.	Leaders arrive and set up. Pray together.
2.00	Children begin to arrive. Register them and send them straight to… **Opening activities.** They choose from the selection round the room.
2.25	Gather together. Welcome. Say who we are and what's going to happen. **Fun challenge.** Award prizes.
2.35	**Main party activity 1** (could be split by age-group)
2.55	Gather together again. **Another fun challenge.** Short and interesting **talk.**
3.10	**Main party activity 2**
3.30	Party tea
3.45	Gather together. Reminder of theme. Invitation to other church activities. **Big game** all together.
4.00	Go home

Main party activity

You could try:

- a hired bouncy castle or ball pool
- team or relay races
- parachute games
- craft or cooking projects
- traditional party games adapted to the theme (e.g. appropriate music for Musical Statues or Pin the Tail on the Comet).

Fun challenges

Doughnuts on a string – Tie three ring doughnuts on a string and tie the string to a pole. Hold the pole up so the doughnuts hang down to mouth level. Volunteers have to eat the doughnuts without using their hands or licking their lips.

Going to the beach – Have a big pile of beach stuff, e.g. Lilo, beach ball, cricket bat, picnic box, deck chair, snorkel, flippers, towel… Challenge a volunteer to carry it all to a certain place ('the beach') in one go.

Newspaper stand – How many people can you get standing on one sheet of newspaper?

Space party

Opening activities

- star potato printing or graffiti wall
- decorating star biscuits
- big junk model of a rocket
- star mobiles
- face-painting: stars and space-travellers.

Talk outline

1. Amazing facts about stars:

- A star is a ball of burning gas. A tiny piece would burn you to death from 200km (130 miles) away ('from here to…').
- The sun is our nearest star – it looks much bigger than other stars because it is closer.
- A car (at 60mph) would take 50 million years to get to the nearest star.
- Planets are made of rock – like our Earth. Nine go round our Sun.

2. Make the solar system getting volunteers to hold up objects. Measure the distance between objects as follows (these are not to scale with the objects themselves):

   Sun (plastic hula hoop) – 4cm – Mercury (tennis ball) – 5cm – Venus (American-style softball) – 8cm – Earth (small football) – 4cm – Mars (large apple) – 1m with Asteroid belt (trouser belt) – Jupiter (big beach ball) – 1.25m – Saturn (beach ball) – 1.5m – Uranus (football) – 3m – Neptune (basketball) – 3m – Pluto (pea)

3. Put up Psalm 147:4 – 'He determines the number of the stars and calls them each by name.'

   The stars we can see are only a tiny, tiny number compared with all the millions of millions in the universe. Isn't it amazing that God knows every one – and at the same time knows each of us!

Creation party

Opening activities

- modelling with Fimo, playdough or clay
- making sweets or peppermint creams
- junk models
- mobiles of the six days of creation
- face-painting and/or hair-braiding to look like animals and plants

Main activities

Divide into six groups. Allocate each group one day of the creation narrative. They must fill a cardboard poster with whatever God made on that day. Use coloured paper, magazine and catalogue pictures, scissors and glue.

Talk outline

Use the posters to tell the creation story from Genesis 1:1 – 2:3. Emphasize the repeated refrain: 'God saw all that he had made, and it was very good.'

For a further party on this pattern with a Pentecost theme, see page 49.

4 PASS ON THE MESSAGE

IDEAS FOR TELLING WHAT GOD HAS DONE THROUGH JESUS

The ideas in this section will help you pass on to children the good news of Jesus and what he has done for us. Most of the activities highlight particular aspects of the gospel message. There are also programmes and ideas to give an overview of the big story.

• •

The King who loves us

Age: 0-4

Aim: To find out about Jesus and his love for us

These toddler service programme outlines provide suggestions for twenty minutes of songs, story, prayer and chat followed by an activity.

Jesus met the children

Story:	Luke 18:15-17. Tell it from a young child's point of view.
Point:	To Jesus we are very special. He loves and cares for us.
Prayers:	Children in different parts of the world; children who are sad, lonely or ill.
Song:	'Jesus, Jesus, here I am.'
Activity:	Paper children cut out and ready for children to draw faces on and stick on clothes. Write 'Jesus, Jesus here I am' on one side.

Jesus met Zacchaeus

Story:	Luke 19:1-9. Part-act it out – climbing up on a chair as a tree and using props such as toy money and food to pass round.
Point:	Zacchaeus was special to Jesus. Jesus knew all about him.
Prayers:	Being naughty and saying sorry; Jesus knows and loves us.
Songs:	'Now Zacchaeus was a very little man', 'Jesus' love is very wonderful.'
Activity:	Zacchaeus bookmark. Children draw the face and stick the leaves on the tree.

Jesus is the greatest

Story:	Luke 19:28-40. Compare with special occasions and visitors.
Point:	Jesus is the greatest – people sang and were happy when he came.
Prayers:	Praising Jesus.
Song:	'Thank you Lord for this fine day' (… for loving us, … you are the best).
Activity:	Make newspaper palm branches, flags and banners.

Church stories Age: 0-4

Aim: To introduce gospel truth through early experiences of church

Use Duplo or Playmobil to tell stories about the life of an imaginary church. Don't just focus on the church building, but create other parts of the town in which it is situated that are appropriate for each story you do. Have some regular characters who reappear each time, and introduce new ones. Encourage the children to participate in the story-making. This will help them process their early experiences of church and talk about aspects of Christian life. Here are examples of storylines:

- Wendy (the guard on a train) and Rosie (her daughter) are invited to church for the first time. Rosie keeps asking 'Why?' about everything that happens.
- The church heating fails at Christmas – Wendy invites them to the train shed instead for the service – they act out the Christmas story.
- Wendy hears about Jesus forgiving people. She forgives Charlie (the driver) for deliberately running over the sandwiches she'd left on the line.
- Wendy chats to Charlie about Jesus. He wants to come to church to hear more.

• •

Treasure box Age: 0-10

Aim: To build anticipation of a story and recap previous episodes

Have a special box which a child opens at the beginning of each session to discover an item you will use in relating that day's part of the Jesus story, e.g. a nappy (Jesus' birth), a fishing net (call of the fishermen), roof tile (healing of the paralyzed man). Each time the box can also contain the items from the previous sessions – so you can use this as a recap on the story so far. Keep it quick.

The wheels on the donkey

Age: 0-6

Aim: To learn and celebrate the story of Jesus' birth

Work with the children on your own song to tell the Christmas story, using the tune of 'The wheels on the bus' (in many secular songbooks and tapes for young children). Make sure your main point or message is included and you are accurate to the Bible – it matters for young children as much as older ones. For example, you might start as follows:

1. Joseph and Mary went tramp, tramp, tramp… all day long.
2. Baby Jesus was born in Bethlehem, Bethlehem, Bethlehem… long, long ago.
3. The sheep in the field went baa, baa, baa… all night long.
4. The angel in the field said, 'Your King's born!'… 'Go and see!'

Find an occasion, e.g. a Christmas Day service, when others can join in 'their' song.

THINK!

When we are engaging in evangelism, we need to remember that children have some natural limitations. For example, many of them will not yet be able to work with abstract ideas such as guilt or freedom. Rather, they need to think about concrete, everyday things such as 'feeling sad', 'saying sorry' and 'being friends'. For example, it is better for us to offer children the opportunity to 'say sorry to God for the things we have done wrong' rather than use language like 'confessing our sins'. Likewise, we may want to encourage a child to become 'a friend of Jesus' rather than 'committing their life to Jesus'.

Party time! Age: 0-14

Aim: To tell the whole gospel story over a number of weeks

This is a basic programme outline which can be used in any setting, e.g. sermons, short talks at a club, or as home group material.

1. *Christmas party* – Isaiah 7:14; Matthew 1:23. Whatever the season, get right into the festive spirit with trees, decorations and presents to celebrate Jesus, God with us.
2. *Wedding at Cana* – John 2:1-12. Have wedding food, dress up and focus on verse 11 that this was Jesus' first miracle and it showed his disciples who he really was.
3. *The great banquet* – Luke 14:15-24. Make sure you send out invitations to this session and think together about how God has prepared a banquet for us. 'Everything is ready!'

4. *Breakfast on the beach* – John 21:1-13. Get shorts and shades, buckets and spades, and even a barbecue for some beach fun. Jesus died and came alive again. Death is defeated.
5. *Cocktail party* – Galatians 5:22. Prepare drinks with different flavours. Jesus' followers are 'flavoured' with God's Spirit. The 'flavour' is fruity – as described in Galatians.
6. *Heaven's party* – Revelation 21. Look at the picture given of heaven. What will life with God for ever be like? Emphasize that God will be our God and we will be his people.

• •

Jesus has power Age: 0-14

Aim: To explore who Jesus is over a number of weeks

This basic programme outline looks at incidents in Mark where Jesus revealed his power and left people wondering 'Who is this man?' However you use and adapt it, take care to have this emphasis – 'So who is Jesus? What does this tell us about him? How do you react to him now?'

- Jesus has power over illness (Mark 1:29-39). Jesus heals many people.
- Jesus has power over sin (Mark 2:1-12). Jesus heals the paralyzed man.
- Jesus has power over nature (Mark 4:35-41). Jesus calms the storm.
- Jesus has power over death (Mark 5:21-42). Jesus raises Jairus's daughter.

• •

Good news Age: 7-14

Aim: To introduce a session about Jesus

This advert sketch requires two actors. Introduce it with 'And now for a commercial break'. Al and Bo both enter with newspapers. They sit and read. Al gradually becomes more and more miserable, eventually sliding to the floor sobbing. At the same time Bo is increasingly happy, making excited exclamations and hooting with laughter. As Al suddenly stops crying and gets up to see what Bo is reading, a 'voiceover' says 'For a really good news experience, read the *Daily...*' At that exact point Al snatches away Bo's paper to reveal that she is actually reading a Bible behind it. Both freeze.

Parable of the missing bit

Age: 4-10

Aim: To show that Jesus loves people who do wrong

To prepare, make a simple jigsaw for each group. These can be any size or you can all work together. Put coloured spots on the backs of the pieces to identify each jigsaw. Hide the pieces round the space so they can be found without too much difficulty. But take one piece from each jigsaw and put them together in a place that is much harder to find.

Give each group a colour of spot to look for and ask them all to find and complete their jigsaws. At some point, frustration should develop. You could decide in the end to give a hint as to where the last pieces are hidden.

Ask the children how they felt when they were looking for the last piece and when they found it. Read Luke 15:8-10. Was that like the game? Read Luke 15:1-3 to see why Jesus told that story. Some people thought Jesus should not share a meal with anyone bad. Jesus wanted them to know that he especially cared for people who did wrong and wanted to get them put right with God.

People who said 'yes' to Jesus Age: 4-14

Aim: To explore Jesus' life and how we can respond to him

This activity looks at people who said 'yes' to Jesus. Each one recognized some part of God's nature in Jesus: his authority, his love, his acceptance, his power to change. They showed their responses in different ways – weeping, giving cash handouts, running seven miles. This theme gives an unpressurized invitation to children to make their own responses to the God who has come looking for us in Jesus.

1. Mary (Luke 1:26-56). Said 'yes' to God's plan – for her and the world.
2. A paralyzed man (Luke 5:17-26). Said 'yes' to Jesus' authority.
3. A sinful woman (Luke 7:36-50). Said 'yes' to Jesus' forgiveness.
4. A man with a skin disease (Luke 17:11-19). Said 'yes' to Jesus – personally.
5. Zacchaeus (Luke 19:1-9). Said 'yes' to Jesus and changed.
6. A criminal (Luke 23:32-49). Said 'yes' to Jesus – for ever.
7. Cleopas and friend (Luke 24:13-36). Said 'yes' to the risen Lord.

THINK!

One of the most amazing things about the gospel story is that we are part of it. The story that we read in the Bible doesn't end there: it carries on into history in the lives of those who continue to follow Jesus. Each of us has a personal story of faith which tells how we came to know God and how we are continuing to get to know him more day by day. In that personal story there may be smaller stories of times when we have been helped or even rescued by God; when prayers have (or haven't) been answered; when we have moved on in our understanding of who God is and what he has done; when we have felt particularly close to or far from God, or when we have been challenged by the gospel to change the way we live. Whatever our personal faith story, we can share it with children to help them to begin to piece together how God works in the lives of those who follow him.

Pentecost party Age: 4-10

Aim: To introduce the Holy Spirit and what he does

This party is based on the outline on pages 43-44.

Opening activities

- hand-made cards: stamp-printing, embossing, colouring a printed card
- decorating a big birthday cake for everyone to share later
- glass-painting – nightlight holders
- jewellery or friendship bracelets.

Suggested talk outline

1. Talk about birthdays – who likes them? Is there a birthday today? Explain the party today is to celebrate Pentecost – the church's birthday. In honour of birthdays we make cakes.
2. Make a cake using a microwave oven. Follow the recipe, demonstrating in front of the children. While mixing explain that Pentecost is when we celebrate God's Holy Spirit coming to be with God's people – the church – all the time. The Holy Spirit comes to make people how they were meant to be.
3. As the cake is cooking in the microwave ask someone to come and briefly watch what is happening. Can you see the microwaves? How do we know they are doing anything? We can see that the mixture has changed from being gooey to being a sponge cake. When God's Holy Spirit comes to be with his people he changes them, too. You can't see the Holy Spirit, just as you couldn't see the microwaves, but you can see that people change. God promises that everyone can have his Spirit. It's one of the things that Jesus made possible for us. Church is for people who know they can't live as they were meant to without God and his Spirit.

Peter scenes Age: 4-10

Aim: To get an overview of Jesus' life and explore the Trinity

Ask someone artistic to create A3-size drawings with simple bold lines showing the following scenes from Peter's life:

1. Peter fishing from a boat (Luke 5:4)
2. Peter called by Jesus (Mark 3:16-17)
3. Peter amazed at Jesus (Mark 4:37)
4. Peter denying Jesus (Mark 14:66-72)
5. Peter forgiven (John 21:15-19)
6. Peter preaching at Pentecost (Acts 2:14)

Lay them out round the room with equipment for a different painting method by each one (use ready-mixed paint for the first four):

- brushes – lots of different shapes and sizes
- finger paint (thickened with PVA), plenty of warm water and soap for washing
- wax candle to draw over the lines, paint thinned with water to brush over it
- a photocopy of the picture cut along the lines to make stencils, sponges to apply paint
- glue, fabric, paper, string for a collage
- glue to spread on, powder paint and glitter to sprinkle over it and shake off.

Work in groups. Use the finished pictures to tell Peter's life story based on the six events shown. This is a good way of introducing the Trinity to children. Peter would have grown up knowing about God and all the great things he had done in the past. Then Peter met Jesus and found that in him he was meeting God face to face: we call Jesus God's Son. When Jesus had died, been raised to life and gone back to be with his Father God, he sent his Holy Spirit to make Peter and the others able to live for him and tell others about him. Now God was as close to Peter as he could possibly be.

. . . .

Stone in the shoe Age: 4-10

Aim: To show that God can put wrong things right

Pretend to go for a walk. Make a show of your foot hurting and what can be causing it. Look in the shoe and find a stone. Read the Bible verse wrapped round it: 'All have turned away … there is no-one who does good, not even one' (Romans 3:12). Make the link with the stone – the things we do wrong hurt God, they hurt other people and they hurt us. Read the other side of the slip of paper: 'As far as the east is from the west, so far has he removed our transgressions from us' (Psalm 103:12). Get rid of the stone – in the same way, Jesus gets rid of the things we have done wrong.

Glimpse of heaven Age: 4-14

Aim: To explore the idea of heaven – life with God for ever

Have a suitcase full of things for a holiday abroad. Include a passport, money, first-aid kit, hankies, teddy or comfort blanket (to cope with the fear of flying), Bible and any other items the children will find funny. Also have a travel brochure.

Say that you've got to dash off on holiday. Decide to check that you've packed your passport. Empty all the stuff out of the case as you look. At this point an accomplice enters and asks where you are going. Be evasive, eventually pointing to the brochure.

The accomplice looks in it, says 'Heaven!' in surprise and then explains why you won't need all those items, reading Revelation 21:3-4 and then John 14:2-3 from the Bible.

- first-aid kit – no pain
- hankies – no tears
- teddy – no dying and no fear
- money – Jesus has already paid for everything
- passport – it isn't who we are or where we come from that will make us able to live with God for ever. It's being Jesus' followers. All we need to say is 'I'm with him.'

Painted gospel Age: 7-14

Aim: To give an overview of the good news

This presentation uses simple painting to help tell the big story of the gospel. Practise beforehand. For the painting surface you will need a large area of paper with a slightly smaller sheet Blu-tacked on top.

1. Talk about the perfect world that God made. Paint grass and flowers along the bottom, a sun and birds in the sky, trees up the sides. In the bottom centre put a stick figure next to the word 'God'. Explain that when God first made people they were best friends. They were together in the beautiful world.

2. Explain that the closeness broke down because people were selfish and did not love God. Use dark colours and greys to paint 'anger', 'lie', 'kill', 'steal' down the middle of the paper, creating a barrier between God and people. Explain that because God is holy and pure he couldn't be near all the mess that sin (that's the wrong stuff) makes. Tear the paper down the middle and then Blu-tack the two halves about 20cm apart from each other.

3. God still loved people. He had a plan to rescue the situation and bring people close to him again. Draw another stick figure that joins 'God' to people. Explain that God sent his Son – Jesus – to be a person on earth to mend the friendship again. Jesus showed people what God is really like. But people didn't like what Jesus said and did. Just as they had rejected God, now they killed Jesus. Paint a black cross over the Jesus figure. Jesus died on the cross.

4. In an amazing way, because Jesus died, the gap between people and God has been bridged. Paint a huge red heart shape over the middle of the cross. God made Jesus alive again. Now he's with God, but he has given his Holy Spirit to be with us. It was because of God's love for us that he couldn't leave the mess. It was because of God's huge love that Jesus died and was made alive again. And it is because of God's huge love that we can now say sorry for all we do that is wrong. God promises to forgive those who are sorry so we can start again, close to God, just as it was in the beginning.

For other gospel overviews see 'The gospel in a nutshell' in *Bringing Children to Faith* by Penny Frank in this series and the song 'Colours of Salvation' by Jim Bailey on the album *Children of the Cross* – wave the appropriately coloured flags as you work through the gospel story as in the song.

Ordinary me Age: 4-14

Aim: To show that God calls ordinary people

Ask three or four adults or young people to be prepared to answer the question: 'How did you come to know Jesus?' Ask them each to think of just two or three key things to say and chat it through beforehand to help them clarify it. Also ask them to bring along any very ordinary but useful item they own – white mug, clear plastic bag, pencil, bucket, piece of string.

Show the children the objects. Then for each one ask the owner what it is and what they do with it. Then ask them the prepared question. You could ask supplementary questions to bring out more of their stories, but keep them short. Read 1 Corinthians 1:26-28. Explain that God asks very ordinary people to be his friends. Whatever other people think of us, God wants us and he will use us for great things. He gives us his Holy Spirit to make that possible. You could go on to look at the ordinary people who became Jesus' followers in the Gospels.

Miracle Maker weekend

Age: 11-14

Aim: To present Jesus' life and build relationships

Hold an Easter weekend event, with something each day for 11-14s. Get the church young people to take as big a part as possible in organizing it – both for themselves and to publicize to others. Get the group to commit themselves to all four events, if possible. You could invite other young teens groups in the area to get involved, too. For example:

- Good Friday – video of *The Miracle Maker*
- Saturday – day out, e.g. theme park or other attraction
- Easter Day – breakfast at a leader's house followed by going to all-age service together
- Easter Monday – run a session like your normal group time as a taster – looking at what difference it makes that Jesus is alive.

THINK!

Put simply, evangelism is the task of telling other people about Jesus Christ, God's Son. Of course, actually doing this is not so simple, but we can't begin until we are sure what it is we have to say.

'For God so loved the world that he gave his one and only Son, so that whoever believes in him shall not perish but have eternal life.' John 3:16

Think through that statement – it's fantastic! There are so many exciting ideas and thoughts in it for us: 'God so loved the world', 'he gave', 'whoever believes', 'shall not perish', 'eternal life'. Come back to this verse again. And again. Why not write it out and put it somewhere where you'll see it over the next few weeks?

Question of identity

Age: 11-14

Aim: To explore who Jesus is

Work on the following dramatic scenes involving the lives of 11-14s. Ideally break into groups and then show each other what you've done. Each group can work on more than one scene.

- A gets really into something and doesn't do what his/her parents expected.
- B surprises people who wouldn't expect much from someone of his/her age.
- C gets roasted by his/her worried parents.
- D has to go with his/her parents to a big event.
- E tries to explain he/she is innocent but his/her parents can't understand.
- F chooses to do what his/her parents say.

Read Luke 2:41-52. Point out that Jesus experienced what it is like to be 11, 12, 13, 14… That doesn't mean he handled it just like we do. He was different. Get the group to suggest some of the things said in their scenes which might have been said in this incident too. What would not have been said? Use this to explore who Jesus is – a real young person in a human family and at the same time God's Son. This could be turned into a dramatic performance for others.

• •

Crumpled clothes Age: 4-10

Aim: To talk about our need to be put right by God

Have a large basket of unironed clothes. Include some nice clothes and some weird and tasteless ones. Set up an iron and ironing board.

Pick out a few of the clothes and ask who would be prepared to be seen by their friends wearing them. As you start work, show that very crumpled and also slightly creased clothes all need ironing. Make it an interactive question-and-answer time: Which is the worst one? The best? Make the connection: sometimes we are like this, all messed up. We might feel pretty sorted, but actually even slightly 'creased' people are not good enough for God. Read or explain the truth of Romans 3:23-26. God wants us perfect – and he can do the straightening out, however grungy or crumpled we think we are.

5 LISTEN OUT

IDEAS FOR ENCOURAGING CHILDREN'S RESPONSES TO GOD

The ideas in this section give opportunities for children to respond to God in ways appropriate to them. They provide a framework within which the children can express their own response in prayer, activity, words or practical action.

Thank you prayers Age: 0-6

Aim: To thank God together

Ask the children to think of things or people they want to thank God for. Use the following pattern of response – practise it first:

Child: For sausage and beans

Leader: We really want to say,

Everyone: Thank you!

This works well in an all-age setting provided everyone can hear the prayer ideas. Use a roving microphone if possible.

Bubble prayers Age: 0-6

Aim: To pray for people

Use bubbles to pray for people – either those present or others they suggest. Each time you blow a bubble say 'Who's this bubble for?' When a child suggests a name, pray for that person in a way that fits with your theme. For example, after hearing about Jesus' love for all people, pray 'Thank you Jesus for loving (*name*)'. Let older children have a go at blowing bubbles too. Toddlers will enjoy playing with empty, clean bubble pots and loops.

Next time Age: 0-14

Aim: To encourage children to come to another event

Have a spot where you say what other activities and events the children can come to. For example, at an all-age service give the date of the next similar service and a hint of the story or theme. At a one-off event, talk about any regular children's groups and explain how to come and try them; also give the date of the next special event. Do it in a fun way, for example:

- *Into the box* – Use the *Treasure Box* idea (page 46), e.g. at an all-age service or toddler group, but put the item(s) into the box at the end of the previous session as a hint of what's coming next time.
- *Balloon burst* – Write the information about the next event on slips of paper, e.g. date, time, venue, title, one or two things that will be happening. Put them in balloons and blow up extras, too. Ask children to burst the balloons, to find the information and to read it out.
- *Gunge bowl* – Like *Balloon burst* but put the slips in plastic film canisters in a bucket of thick green custard.
- *Ad* – Get some young people to devise an advert for the next event or for your regular group meeting, based on a well-known TV commercial.

Top moment Age: 0-10

Aim: To respond to a Bible story

Ask each child to draw a picture of their favourite moment from the Bible story. Encourage leaders to see this as a vital time to chat about what was said, asking simple questions like 'Why did you like that?' 'Why is Jesus smiling?' You might need to train your leaders in using open-ended questions rather than closed ones with yes/no answers. Be careful not to judge or be disrespectful of what the children have produced, but do gently clarify any major points they have clearly misheard or misunderstood. Leaders could also draw their own pictures as a way of chatting about their own response to the story.

If you repeat the activity, vary the drawing materials, e.g. crayons, chalks, overhead projector pens and acetates. If you follow the Bible story with a craft activity, try to make it something where the children have at least a little freedom of expression and use it in a similar way.

Sound and verse Age: 0-10

Aim: To encourage a range of honest responses

Read a verse of a psalm which expresses a response to the content of your session. Work together to devise sound effects and actions to go with the verse. You could do this in small groups and then all do your actions and sounds together, repeating the verse three or four times. Get louder and softer if appropriate. There may be a verse or phrase from the Bible material for the session which you can use, or try one of the following:

- Psalm 16:1 – 'Keep me safe, O God…'
- Psalm 42:1 – Longing for God
- Psalm 100:1-2 – 'Sing for joy to the Lord…'
- Psalm 106:1-2 – 'Praise the Lord!'
- Psalm 121:1-2 – Looking to God for help

In on the ground floor

Age: 0-14

Aim: To help ownership of an event

Invite children to help you with the practical preparation for an event. Look for tasks where this is possible – even if it takes more time than doing it yourself – for example, making and delivering invitations, preparing food, getting the space ready, choosing music or games, preparing craft materials. This will help them own the event or group and is a good way in to getting their suggestions and involving them in planning future events. Don't just involve the children you know best. Someone who's only been once may be pleased to be asked their opinion about the next event and will get stuck in to helping as a first response to their welcome by the group.

Preparation and clearing away are good times to chat with children and young people of any age.

Musical additions Age: 0-14

Aim: To update old songs using more relevant words

Encourage the children to adapt songs in a way appropriate to their age. For younger children ask for suggestions to use in old favourites like 'Thank you Lord for…'. Several of the songs on the CD *God's Wonderful World* by Julia Plaut (Kingsway) are good for this, for example use the song 'If I go climbing' to explore places where the children go and know God is with them.

For an older age-group, ask them to suggest new verses for songs such as 'We are marching in the light of God' (Siyahamba) or 'In my life, Lord, be glorified'. If they do not usually sing in your regular setting, use their ideas in an all-age service.

'Think about' box Age: 0-14

Aim: To think and talk further after a service

At all-age services (and others, too) have a box on the church notice sheet with questions to think about. Word these in simple language so families can easily use them if they want to chat further about the service at home. You could have a question about the content of the story, something applying it today and an open-ended challenge. For example, for a service on the rich young ruler (Luke 18:18-30) think about:

- What question did the man in today's story ask Jesus? Was it a good one?
- Do you know anyone who's given something up because they follow Jesus?
- Is there anything we need to do about what we've heard this morning?

Bean care Age: 0-14

Aim: To express a desire to keep growing

Give each person a few beans or seeds to plant and grow at home if they want to. On the envelopes write out 2 Peter 3:18. Explain that this is to remind them of the need to keep growing in God's love and knowing Jesus more and more. It is God who brings about that growth in us by his Holy Spirit. We just need to ask him – and to do our part by finding out more about him from the Bible. You can also link this with the parable of the sower (Matthew 13:1-23). Ask informally over the next few weeks how the plants are getting on. If appropriate, ask the group members if they feel God is helping them to grow, too. Are they getting to know Jesus more?

Setting a task like this can especially help those children who learn best by practical action. Here are two more examples:

- What's the most multicoloured thing you can find and bring next week (a reminder of the rainbow and God's patience with us – Genesis 8:21-22)?
- Give each child a bit of cloth with washable red pen marks on to rinse out at home (a reminder of God's forgiveness – Isaiah 1:18).

Prayer request box Age: 0-14

Aim: To pray for children's needs and show care for them

Encourage children, or parents of younger children, to write down any prayer requests they have and put them in the box. Promise that the team will pray about the things they put in the box. Arrange a specific time when you will pray together, rather than leaving it to individual team members.

• •

Prayer basics Age: 0-14

Aim: To introduce children to group prayer

Regularly talk about the basics of prayer. Don't assume that children know how to pray in the way we do in groups and churches. Encourage stillness and quiet, tell them what we are doing when we pray, and encourage respect towards God and to the other people in the group. Encourage the group to think of prayer as being like talking to someone who knows you really well and loves you. You can talk to them honestly and say whatever you want. With younger children you may want to encourage them to put their hands on their laps or together and close their eyes, or look at a particular picture to help them concentrate.

• •

Ask and pray Age: 0-14

Aim: To include children's ideas in a prayer time

Ask the children for ideas of what to pray for. Listen carefully and use what they have said to shape the prayers you lead. At an all-age service, you could make a regular feature of going round with a notebook asking if anyone has things they would like included in the prayers. Then include them.

Pray-it notes Age: 0-14

Aim: To help every child pray

Give the children sticky notes to write or draw their prayers on. Either make suggestions (e.g. something you want God's help for; telling God he's great; something to thank God for) or leave it open. Encourage them to bring the prayers and stick them on a big poster. This could have a key verse from your Bible material written on it, or be a picture poster showing some part of God's creation.

• •

Photo file Age: 0-14

Aim: To pray for children's concerns

Ask the group members to bring along photographs of any people, places or situations they want the group to pray about. These could be of their family and friends or pictures from newspapers or magazines. Sit around the pictures and spend time talking about what is in them and what the prayer need is. Look at the pictures in silence and then lead a prayer asking God to act in those situations.

• •

Shape prayers Age: 4-14

Aim: To pray, remembering the Holy Spirit helps us

Make and cut out flame shapes from red, orange and yellow card. Explain that these are a reminder of the Holy Spirit. He helps us pray. Ask each child to write a one-sentence prayer on a card shape. Get them to bring their flames to the front and stick them on the wall together. The final result looks very effective. If any want to pray something private explain that they can just put a cross on the flame or write their own name.

Use other pre-cut shapes to fit with different Bible passages, e.g. sheep for the parable of the lost sheep (Luke 15:1-7), bricks to pray for your church (Ephesians 2:22).

Mexican wave Age: 4-14

Aim: To praise God

Get the children to do a Mexican wave. Starting at one side of the room, each person stands and raises their arms and then sits again. They should start to rise as soon as they sense the person to their left beginning to move. Aim for a smooth flow round the group. Then try doing it with a repeated chant of praise, e.g. 'Hosanna, hosanna…' which gets louder and louder as the wave goes round. You could end with a clash on a cymbal.

Pick a line Age: 4-14

Aim: To own the words of response songs

Choose a song with good words which relates to your Bible material and expresses a response to God – this could be on CD or a song for the group to sing. After playing or singing it, read through the words and ask children to choose a line or phrase they particularly like. Let any volunteers say what they have chosen and why.

Wandering prayer Age: 4-14

Aim: To help concentration in prayer

Label parts of the room: 'Sorry, Lord', 'Thank you, Lord', 'You're wonderful, Lord', 'Please, Lord'. Encourage people to wander and use the areas for praying in the way shown. If you are in a big space, have a different kind of music playing in each area. Keep space free for people who want to pray in their own way or not to pray.

THINK!

Response to God is a continuing process for all of us. We all need to come back again and again to the wonderful things God has done for us in Jesus and to let them make their impact afresh in our lives. Often we won't recognize all of the response we are making, which includes the work that the Holy Spirit is doing in our lives.

In the same way the Holy Spirit can work in children well before they recognize his power. Be encouraged to look for signs of spiritual life in them. The Holy Spirit will change uncooperative attitudes or a grumpy temper and challenge actions such as swearing and violent reactions. Notice how children ask questions and remember things said many months ago – both signs that God is at work in their lives.

Prayer drill Age: 4-14

Aim: To start off prayer together

This old technique can still be a good way of starting prayers off, especially where some children struggle to keep quiet and still. There are five actions which everyone does as you call out the numbers:

1. Hold left hand out and shake it about.
2. Hold right hand out and shake it as well.
3. Move hands around each other in tight circles.
4. Fold arms. Everyone is quiet. (Say a prayer.)
5. Put hands down.

• •

Question mark group

Age: 7-14

Aim: To help children find out more

Just before your main meeting time, publicize a time and place where children can come to ask questions and talk further about the things you are learning. This could also be a focus for those who are reading the Bible every day to compare notes – perhaps using daily Bible notes. Beware of limiting it to the more academically able children – the aim is to reach the most spiritually hungry.

Q Wall Age: 7-14

Aim: To help group members ask their real questions

Have a large wall space where group members can write up any questions they have about God, the church or just about anything. Make the limits clear – allow funny questions (e.g. What's the fastest cake in the world?) but nothing which is hurtful to anyone else in the group. If wall space is not available, use a roll of paper, portable board or sticky notes which can be removed and replaced.

Either have a regular spot or special event (with guest panel) to tackle the questions, or keep them up and refer to them as part of your regular teaching programme. Be willing to admit when you don't know an answer. Agree that you will all go away and think, and will come back to it another time. Watch out for questions which need individual follow-up.

• •

Time to reflect Age: 7-14

Aim: To allow space for thinking and prayer

Where children have a choice of activities, provide a time-out zone – a quiet corner with comfy cushions and gentle music. With a younger age-group there could also be simple individual activities, e.g. paper and pens or an activity sheet related to the content of the event.

Dear God... Age: 7-14

Aim: To help children pray privately

Invite the children to write letters to God. Put on some background music to give a helpful relaxed atmosphere. Provide paper and envelopes. Have other quiet things to do for those who finish first. Encourage them to seal the letters so they are private. Let them keep them, read them, add to them or start again whenever they want.

● ●

Mail chain Age: 11-14

Aim: To support each other in prayer

Encourage members of the group to pray for each other. They may well like to do this even if they are at a stage of belonging but not yet believing. To pass round prayer needs, you could devise a prayer chain (people phone each other in turn down the chain to pass on news) or some could keep in touch by e-mail.

Lord, our Lord Age: 4-10

Aim: To praise our great God

Read this shortened version of Psalm 8 together. Discuss what it makes you think about God and how you feel about him. Think of words to describe God, e.g. powerful, strong, big. How can these be portrayed in sound? Use percussion instruments to find sounds for each section of the psalm. Put it all together and praise God.

Lord, our Lord,
your greatness is seen in all the world;
your praise reaches up to the heavens;
you are safe and secure from your enemies.

When I look at the sky which you have made,
at the moon and stars which you set in place,
what are we that you think of us?

Yet you crowned us with glory, rulers of everything
you have made;
over all creation,
sheep and cattle, wild animals too,
the birds and the fish,
the creatures in the sea.

Lord, our Lord,
your greatness is seen in all the world.

THINK!

Children's responses to God, or indeed their apparent lack of response, have a big impact on us, the teams working with them. We need to pray for maturity in handling that impact. It is so easy to have mixed motives – longing for children to make steps forward in their faith but partly wanting it so we can feel successful. That becomes a danger when it leads us to pressurize children to make responses in ways that will affirm us by being visible. It can also cause divisions in the team when some are able to talk excitedly of seeing children taking steps forward while others are left feeling they have failed.

We need to help each other deal with these pressures. We need to affirm each other for our faithfulness to God – not for any visible success. We need to keep reminding each other of the nature of children's growth in faith – wonderful and exciting, yes, but often not spoken or seen. We need to pray continually for each other. And we need to have Psalm 115:1 as our motto:

'Not to us, O Lord, not to us
but to your name be the glory,
because of your love and faithfulness.'

Team prayer Age: 0-14

Aim: To pray as a team for the children in your groups

Keep praying as a team for the children you are working with. You could make Ephesians 3:16-19 your team prayer – for them and each other:

'I pray that out of his glorious riches he may strengthen you with power through his Spirit in your inner being, so that Christ may dwell in your hearts through faith. And I pray that you, being rooted and established in love, may have power, together with all the saints, to grasp how wide and long and high and deep is the love of Christ, and to know this love that surpasses knowledge – that you may be filled to the measure of all the fulness of God.'

Pray for eyes to see what God is doing in children's lives. And be encouraged by Ephesians 3:20-21. That's what it's all about.

• •

Diary sheet Age: 0-14

Aim: To reflect back on experiences and learning

Provide a sheet which children of all ages can use to reflect back on the service, event or group time. On a residential event this can be a way of looking back over the day's experiences and learning. Provide spaces for people to draw or write in, such as the following:

- Star spot *(star shape)*
- Worst bit *(bin)*
- Someone I met *(photo outline and space for name under)*
- I learned this about God *(brain shape)*
- I want to say to God *(speech bubble)*

Encourage people to talk about what they have put – but only if they want to. You could use a similar method for getting feedback if people hand the sheets in – but you need to be clear that this is the purpose before they start drawing and writing.

Alternatively, simply provide a blank piece of paper and pen for people to use during a service or event. This could be a regular feature with different suggestions each time about how the sheet might be used.

Pics and prayers Age: 0-14

Aim: To help everyone pray in their own way

Photocopy photographs onto overhead projector slides to reflect the main themes for prayer which you want to include. You could use your own photographs, e.g. of people in church, the local area or the whole group, and also pictures from newspapers and magazines. For the prayer time, play some music which the age-group will connect with and which fits the theme of the prayers: lively, praising or more meditative. Encourage the group to pray silently as you put up the pictures one by one.

Alternatively, for an all-age situation, copy several pictures on to A3 sheets of paper. Give these out to small groups and ask them to pray together using the ideas there.

THINK!

We need to give children opportunities to respond to God in little ways which they understand and can cope with. We might offer the children the opportunity to join in songs about who God is and what he has done for us; to join in prayers saying sorry to God for the things we have done wrong; or to write letters to God about how we feel after hearing a story about Jesus. This type of small activity allows the child to respond to God in a way which:

- is comfortable
- is appropriate to their stage of development in terms of language and faith
- doesn't last too long (avoiding the boredom factor)
- helps him or her to belong to the group
- builds up relationships in the group.

RESOURCES FROM CPAS AND SCRIPTURE UNION

From CPAS

CPAS Code

Growing in Faith Series (CPAS/Scripture Union)

03157	Children Finding Faith	Francis Bridger
85007	Bringing Children to Faith	Penny Frank
18006	The ART of 3-11s	
18007	Who Cares?	Rachel Heathfield
30001	My Place in God's Story	Rachel Heathfield
18003	Time for Children	George Lihou
82010	Families Finding Faith	John Hattam
03576	Seen and Heard	Jackie Cray
18001	Groups Without Frontiers	Phil Moon, Penny Frank, Terry Clutterham

CPAS Sales, Athena Drive, Tachbrook Park, WARWICK CV34 6NG
Tel: (01926) 334242
24-hour Sales Ansaphone: (01926) 335855
E-mail: sales@cpas.org.uk
Web: www.cpas.org.uk

From Scripture Union

ISBN

Growing in Faith Series (CPAS/Scripture Union)

1 85999 323 0	Children Finding Faith	Francis Bridger
1 85999 410 5	Bringing Children to Faith	Penny Frank
1 87679 413 5	Children and the Gospel	Ron Buckland
0 86201 906 0	The Adventure begins	Terry Clutterham
1 85999 525 7	Y God?	Steve Hutchinson
1 85999 096 7	Pick 'n' Mix: over 100 ideas to create programmes for children of all ages	Judith Merrell
1 85999 219 6	Jump! Bible activities for your group aged 5-7	Zoë Crutchley and Veronica Parnell
1 85999 215 3	On your marks! Bible activities for your group aged 8-10	Lorna Sabbagh
1 85999 661 2	Pretty much everything you need to know about working with 8 to10s	Claire Saunders/Hilary Porrit
1 85999 676 0	Kid's Culture: Understanding the world that shapes our children	Nick Harding
1 85999 214 5	Pitstop: Bible activities for your group aged 11-13	Steve Bullock
1 85999 351 6	Generation to Generation: building bridges between churches and schools	Sue Radford et al

Holiday club material (5 day holiday club programme):

1 85999 498 9	Desert Detectives (book and video available)
1 85999 567 5	Seaside Rock (book and video available)

Children's Bible reading resources:

Tiddlywinks (Bible reading and activity resources for pre-school children)
Join in - jump on! (5 to 7 year olds) - 6 books, each containing 50 days of Bible Reading material.
Snapshots (8 to10 year olds) - published quarterly.
One Up (11 to 14 year olds) - published quarterly.
SALT (Sharing And Learning Together) resources: SALT 3 to 4+, SALT 5 to 7+, SALT 8 to 10+, SALT 11 to 13+.
SALT All Ages. A4 leaders and children's magazines published quarterly.

All these resources are available from your local Christian bookshop or from Scripture Union Mail Order,
PO Box 5148 Milton Keynes MLO, MK2 2YX
Tel: 08450 706006
Fax: 01908 856020
Email: subs@scriptureunion.org.uk
Web: www.scriptureunion.org.uk

BIBLICAL INDEX

You can use the ideas in **Mission Possible** *to teach a variety of Bible passages,*
but the passages specifically mentioned are these:

AGE-GROUP INDEX

Many of the activities in **Mission Possible** *can be used or adapted to fit most age-groups, but these are the activities recommended for the following age-groups:*

Growing in Faith series

Three books for all those involved in children's evangelism. The books work together and complement each other, providing a 'head, heart and hands' approach to the subject of child faith development. Written by experts in their field, the series will equip churches with a comprehensive training resource for children's workers.

Children Finding Faith: *Exploring a child's response to God*
Rev Dr Francis Bridger

This revised, expanded version of a popular book examines accepted studies of child development alongside the theological issues relating to children. Children Finding Faith follows the development of two children from birth to adolescence, charting the characteristics of their emotional and spiritual growth. New chapters look at social context, the practical implications of children's work and worship.

£6.99, B format pb, 224 pp   1 85999 323 0 (SU)   1 902041 10 0 (CPAS)

Bringing Children to Faith: *Training adults in evangelism with children*
Penny Frank

This training manual will enable you to think through the principles of good practice for evangelism with children, and implement them in your children's work. In workbook format, Bringing Children to Faith contains photocopiable pages and suggestions for group discussion and activity. Use this resource to plan a series of workshops for your church children's team, a training day or to help you as you develop a whole church strategy for children's evangelism.

£7.50, A4, 48pp   1 85999 410 5 (SU)   1 8976 6093 6 (CPAS)

Mission Possible: *Ideas and resources for children's evangelism*
Various

Mission Possible is a ready-to-use resource book full of ideas and activities for use with children. Arranged in age-group sections, ranging from crèche through to early teens, activities are relevant to children's age and level of development. Drawn from the experience of Scripture Union and CPAS children's workers, these tried and tested activities will enable you to put into practice some of the ideas outlined in the other two books.

£7.50, A4, 64pp   1 85999 411 3 (SU)   1 902041 05 4(CPAS)

You can obtain any of the above books through your local Christian bookshop, via christianbookshop.com or (in the UK) direct from:

Scripture Union Mail Order PO Box 5148 MILTON KEYNES MLO, MK2 2YX Tel: **08450 706006** Fax: 01908 856020
CPAS Sales Athena Drive Tachbrook Park WARWICK CV34 6NG Tel/24 hour voicemail: **01926 458400**

For overseas sales, contact your national Scripture Union office.